INTRODUCTION............................

BREAD...9

SWEETS 24

Introduction

If you have purchased this book under the pretense that it is of recipes for those of us who suffer from sensitivity to gluten, then I strongly suggest you request your money returned, though there are certainly recipes here within that meet that bar, that is not the main purpose of these writings, this is a book about a journey to find alternatives and many of those alternatives include the enhancement of recipes with gluten.

The need to lose weight and keep it off has been a struggle for me all my adult life, as it may be for you. I've done all the popular diets, and (probably like you) I've lost and regained weight over and over again, this became especially critical when I developed type 2 diabetes. The question I began to ask myself was why do I flirt with success and always fail to carry through. After a period of examination what I discovered was that most diets severely limit ingestion of baked goods, and for me that was not a sustainable option, I'd lose weight and then start eating bread, cookies and doughnuts and low and behold the weight would be back on. So I sought to find some sort of replacement, an alternative, that would allowed me to control calories and carbohydrates, both the enemy of a diabetic. My path took many bends, soy flour and almond flour were both explored and rejected for one reason or another (I simply can't abide the taste of soy flour) eventually my quest lead me into the use of oat flour as a replacement for wheat, this eventually lead me to the creation of these recipes as a means to assist in my weight control. I still struggle with my weight, and still on occasion wander from this path (it is extremely difficult to convince a restaurant that they should allow you to bring you own biscuits). But when I do gain a few pounds the close adherence to these recipes for a week or 2 and I'm back to where I should be, to date I've lost 40 pounds and have keep it away.

Oat flour by itself does not make a good material to be used in the baking arts; it does not contain enough gluten to produce bread (for example) that will rise properly. In order to accomplish this age old feat, oat flour must be supplemented, the most obvious material to accomplish this is vital wheat gluten; the question was the proportion of oat flour to gluten. The discovery of this relationship was an interesting journey in experimentation, starting with a1 cup oat flour to 1 cup gluten proportion, which produced a rather tough unforgiving material that had a very off taste. Eventually I was able to determine that the most optimum relationship was 1 cup oat flour to around .38 cups of gluten (about 6 tablespoons), at least for bread, and that these proportion where NOT optimum for everything I was making, thus more experiments and more failures but eventual I was able to determine the proper oat flour to gluten relationship to all the thing I wanted to make.

Do not think of the recipes contained here within as the end all of what can be done with baking with oat flour, rather these recipes are published to help stimulated you to create your own, for example surly the recipes I've included in the area of puff pastry are not the only ones that can be done in this media. Some that you come up with will work, some will not.

There are many factors that dictate how bread (or any other yeast based baked product) rises. In the case of the recipes in this book you will find that the amount of yeast may look excessive. And in some cases that may prove true, the quality of your wheat gluten and its moister content seems to be major contributors here. I have had the experience of using lower quality gluten that took 2 full tablespoons of yeast to get a decent rise, and then switched to higher quality gluten that caused the rise to be too much accelerated thus requiring me to cut the amount of yeast to 1 tablespoon. The lesson here is to pay attention to what your material are telling you, and adjust the recipes accordingly. The same is true of water, the amounts listed work excellently for my location however the dryness of the oat flour and gluten the amount of moisture in the air and other factors can affect this. The timing of the baking can also be a bit of an issue, gas, electric, propane even a wood fire are all baking options and all heat differently. The stove used to develop these recipes (for the ones baked in an oven) was brand new when I started this effort and is an electric model. Your oven may not be as well insulated as mine (or indeed it may be better), so again pay attention to what the materials are telling you, if I've given a baking time of 25 – 30 minutes but the bead is still raw in the middle then you may want to, in general, add some extra baking time to all of these recipes, if it's been burned, back off a bit.

Remember the recipes contain no artificial preservatives, if left in a warm moist environment they will spoil and do so quickly. Always store these bake goods in the refrigerator and understand that they do have a limited shelf life.

On the use of a bread machine

In reviewing the recipes contained in this book you will note the use of a bread machine as the means to knead dough, this is certainly not a requirement, you may knead these dough's by hand. I'm just one of those folks that tend to under knead dough so for me the invention of the bread machine was a god send, it provides a sure method to produce well kneaded dough or to easily mixed recipes and to do so unattended. All recipes listed here that use a bread machine call for you to only process the dough to point that it begins to go into its rise cycle then remove the dough to use in whatever means the recipe calls for, you may allow the bread machine to complete its cycle through baking, this will work, but you may find that the amount of yeast will produce a dough much to active for your machine. The first time I did this it literally pushed the lid of the bread machine open, it was a very interesting mess. I make no suggestion as to the make or model you should chose, I've used several over the course of developing these recipes, the only requirement is that it have a quick, or dough cycle and most modern models have this option.

Yogurt

Yogurt can be a reasonable replacement for fat in many recipes but its not suitable for all types of recipes, for example I would not add it to the sourdough deep fry batter, but it is great as a replacement for fat in the sourdough doughnuts. At present I am using Dannon's Fit and Light, Vanilla yogurt® because of its relatively low calorie and reasonable carbohydrate count. But I would most definitely shop around as new products come on line all the time and something with a better count could show up any day. I've considered the possibility of making my own yogurt, using oat milk as the base material. A yogurt based on oat milk would have a fraction of the calories and carbohydrates as standard yogurt. I've conducted some initial experiments, but as of yet have not produced a reasonable substitute, I will report my results on the oat flour baking web site.

Butter (Spread)

Butter can have a place in a low carbohydrate diet; however the calories are way too high for a diet that seeks to limit both calories and carbohydrates a substitute is required. As of today I have found that Brummel & Brown Spread® (made with Natural Yogurt) seems to provide good taste with limited calories and carbohydrates. But again this is today, tomorrow something else may come on the market and I would switch (and modify the counts on the spreadsheet where I calculate these things, this spreadsheet is available for your use on line).

Egg Substitute

I don't wish that there be any confusion over this term, it is used widely to refer to everything from banana based vegan egg replacements to flax seed and water combinations, the references in this book are not to these materials. This reference is to the various products out there based on real egg, but lacking the yolk, such as Egg Beaters®. These days there are a number of these products on the market, and I have no preference for any special one. Only that is have the lowest calorie and carbohydrate count that I can find.

On the consumption of Fried foods

As with most things fried foods are ok, but ok in moderation only, they should not be a staple in your diet. However you can reduce the negative effects of deep frying food by frying in small batches that allows the temperature of the oil to remain as close set temperature as possible, and draining very well. The idea is that the oil should penetrate into the dough as little as possible as penetration of the oil will add calories to the food. Also use vegetable oil (Canola oil for example) rather that shortening or lard.

Health Benefits

The health benefits of oats have touted heavily over the years in the popular press, in general they can be divided into a few categories:

Heart:
There seems to be a significant amount of literature concerning oats and the reduction of cholesterol. In general this boils down to the dietary fiber found in this grain. The process by which this occurs is well known in science circles, but less known outside of academia. As oats are digested the soluble fiber breaks down into a gel within the digestive tract, this gel has the ability to absorb bad cholesterol (LDL) while allowing the good cholesterol (HDL) to be processed, and the result is that cholesterol is controlled. This process also slows the absorption of carbohydrates, making oats more diabetic friendly. This soluble fiber can also help with hypertension, or high blood pressure.

Cancer:
□ **Insoluble fiber**
Oats contain this material, which will absorb water and help with the movement of food through your system, this can help lower the risk of bowel cancer (such as colon cancer).

□ **Beta Glucan**
this is a bio-defense modifier which can help you with a stronger immune system.

□ **Vitamins and Minerals**
Oats provide a source of Iron, Zinc, Selenium, and Vitamin E.

□ **Phytochemicals**
Yes there are chemicals in oats; some like phytoestrogens (lignans) can help to fight hormone related diseases (like prostate cancer).

Weight control:
The soluble fiber contained in oats (and the associated gel formed during digestion) have one additional benefit worth mentioning, that being that the viscosity of the contains of the stomach is increased, this contributes to an individual's feeling of fullness, and it part explains why switching from wheat to oats has had the impact on my weight that it has had, not only are the calories and carbohydrates lower, but I'm eating less because I feel full quicker. There are also studies that indicate that the protein found in oats it on par (from a quality perspective) with the protein found in soy, and is equal to meat, milks and eggs.

Nutritional value:
The internet is a most wondrous invention, it decimates information far and wide, it also can be the cause of confusion, and a great example is the nutritional value of oat flour. A search in reputable search engine will tell you that the calorie count is 300 calories a cup, or 350 or 404; same with carbohydrates those numbers range from 39 – 65. For the purposes of preparing this book (and because these were the numbers on the first packages of oat flour I purchased)

I've gone with 312 calories and 48 carbohydrates. However I recognize that some of you might want to adjust those numbers to some you are more familiar with, so I have posted a spreadsheet on the books web site (www.oatflourbaking.com) that will allow you to enter values of your own and automatically adjust the nutritional value of all of these recipes. This spreadsheet is protected; the password is OatMilk entered as one word and mind the capital letters.

Sources

These days there are numerous where you can obtain both oat flour and vital wheat gluten no longer are these substances the private domain of the health food store (at health food store prices). Most well-appointed US grocery store carry Bob's Red Mill products and Bob's produces both of these materials. Indeed the bulk area of a chain store in my area carries both at a very reasonable price. If you are connected to the internet (and are not averse to purchasing off the net) you can find many sources, for example Honeyville.com,arrowheadmills.com or grainmillers.com there are many more and it pays to shop around. Because I do a lot a baking with these materials I tend to purchase them in bulk, 50 pounds of oat flour and gluten in 3.5 pound sealed cans (I no longer buy gluten in 25 pound bags, as the ratio of oat flour to gluten is about .38's of a cup of gluten to a cup of oat flour for most of my baking so it tends to last a lot longer and can eventually go bad). Oat flour too can go rancid so don't buy more than a months' supply. If you are one of the more handy types you might try making your own.

Making your own vital wheat gluten is probably beyond most individuals area of expertise, though it may be possible to extract the gluten from wheat flour by forming a dough of wheat flour and water and then kneading it under multiple exchanges of cold water to liberate the gluten from the starch, then drying and grinding the resulting sticky mass that is produced. I've not gone to this extreme; at least not yet, as I've stated above vital wheat gluten is available in many super markets and certainly purchasable from various companies on the internet. Oat flour on the other hand can be economically produced in the home, by a couple of techniques.

Groats:
Groats are the hulled grain of the oat they are very hard and (because of this) can be processed as you would wheat in a home grinding mill. The resulting flour will not be quite as fine as what you purchase (the commercial grinding is not as simple as this), but it will be usable.

Oatmeal:
A more user friendly process is to use common oat meal, however one should never ever use instant oat meal, use rolled oats and simply process them in either a blender or food processor until they reach flour like consistency. This gives the individual the option of making as much or as little oat flour as you wish. Store you're newly made oat flour (from either technique) in a sealed container, refrigeration is not required. So let's start baking!

Bread

Ah the staff of life. For those on a low carbohydrate diet bread is not usually something they can include in their standard fair, small wonder as the average piece of white bread contains about 70 calories and around 12.5 grams of carbohydrates whole wheat is a bit better in the calorie area with 64 calories, but has 14 grams of carbohydrates. My basic oat flour bread beats them both at 62.2 calories and a low 7.2 grams of carbohydrates (half that if you cut it in quarter inch slices) thus permitting perhaps two slices a day. This bread, and its variations, also has a labor saving aspect in that there is no need to do two risings of the dough, a single rising in the bread pan is all that is required. My initial experiments used granulated sugar that produced uneven rising with large gaps in the structure and a grainy appearance, switching to honey magically solved this problem.

Stacks of English muffins with all of their nook and cranny goodness

Basic Bread

This bread recipe is what started this whole experiment, I wanted to know if this was even possible, and if so would it taste good, well its possible and it tastes wonderful. This is excellent bread, keep it in your refrigerator, not only will it extend its keep time, but will also firm it up for easier slicing. It makes a superior toast.

1 cup water
¼ cup egg substitute
1 tablespoon Spread
1 teaspoon salt
3/4 cup vital wheat gluten
2 cups oat flour
1 tablespoon honey
2 tablespoon yeast

Pre-heat oven to 350 degrees, add ingredients in order to bread machine set to quick dough mode and run it to mix and knead. Remove the dough from the machine and place on a flat surface that has been dusted with a bit of oat flour and roll it up tightly, place in a bread pan sprayed with a bit of cooking spray. Cover and place in warm place until the dough has risen about an inch above the rim of the bread pan bake for 25 - 30 minutes. Remove from the oven and place on cooling rack. Makes 18 ½ inch slices

Calorie Count:	
Egg substitute –	30
Gluten –	360
Oat Flour –	624
Honey –	60
Spread –	45
Total:	1119
Per slice:	62.2
Carbohydrates Count:	
Egg substitute –	1
Gluten –	18
Oat Flour –	96
Honey –	15
Spread –	0
Total:	130
Per slice:	7.2

Dinner Rolls

These remind me of the great dinner rolls made by my mother years ago on a small farm in central Wisconsin; I think of her whenever I bake these.

1 cups water
¼ cup egg substitute
1 tablespoon Spread
1 teaspoon salt
3/4 cup vital wheat gluten
2 cups oat flour
1 tablespoon honey
2 tablespoon yeast
2 teaspoons Spread

Heat you oven to 375 degrees, add ingredients in order to bread machine run machine in quick mode. When the machine stops remove the dough. Shape dough into 18 equal rolls and place in a large cake pan or lasagna pan (that has been sprayed with cooking spray). Cover pan and place in warm location; allow to rise until double in size that could take up to 1 ½ hours, place the roll in the oven and bake for 30 minutes. Remove the baked rolls and place on rack to cool. While still hot brush about 2 teaspoons of Spread on the top surface of the rolls. This recipe will make about 18 rolls.

Calorie Count:	
Egg substitute –	30
Gluten –	360
Oat Flour –	624
Honey –	60
Spread –	45
Spread –	30
Total:	1149
Per Roll:	63.8
Carbohydrates Count:	
Egg substitute –	1
Gluten –	18
Oat Flour –	96
Honey –	15
Spread –	0
Spread –	0
Total:	130
Per Roll:	7.2

Bare Essential Bread

Only those things needed to make a loaf, and nothing else.

1 ¼ cup of water
1 teaspoon salt
3/4 cup vital wheat gluten
2 cups oat flour
1 tablespoon honey
2 tablespoon yeast

Pre-heat the oven to 350 degrees, place the ingredients into your bread machine in the order listed, set the machine to quick mode and process. When complete remove to a flat surface that has been dusted with oat flour. Knead lightly and shape into a loaf, place in a bread pan (which has been lightly sprayed with cooking spray. Cover and allow to rise until the dough is about 1 inch above the lip of the bread bake for 25 – 30 minutes. Slice into ½ inch slices, the recipe will make about 18 ½ inch slices.

Calorie Count:	
Gluten –	360
Oat Flour –	624
Honey –	60
Total:	1044
Per Slice:	58.0
Carbohydrates Count:	
Gluten –	18
Oat Flour –	96
Honey –	15
Total:	129
Per Slice:	7.2

Hoagie Rolls

The best for meat ball sandwiches.

1 recipe of Bare Essential Bread

Pre-heat the oven to 350 degrees, prepare the bread as directed in the Bare Essential Bread recipes. After the bread machine finishes kneading remove the dough to a flat surface dusted with oat flour, roll into a rope about 16 inches long, cut into 8 2 inch pieces. Roll each piece into a thin oval about 6 inches long and about 1 inch wide. Place on a cookie sheet lightly sprayed with cooking spray, cover and let rise till double in size. Spray the rolls very lightly with cooking spray and bake for 25 – 30 minutes. Recipe will make 8 loafs.

Calorie Count:	
Gluten –	360
Oat Flour –	624
Honey –	60
Total:	1044
Per loaf:	130.5
Carbohydrates Count:	
Gluten –	18
Oat Flour –	96
Honey –	15
Total:	129
Per loaf:	16.1

Hamburger Buns

This recipe makes 12 great burger buns, to drive down the calorie count even more make these using the bare essentials bread recipe.

1 ½ cups of water
1 tablespoon honey
1 teaspoon salt
1 tablespoon olive oil
¾ cup vital wheat gluten
2 cups oat flour
2 tablespoons yeast

Pre-heat your oven to 350 degrees. Place the ingredients in the order listed into you bread machine, select a quick bread cycle and process until the kneading cycle stops. Remove the dough from the machine and place onto a flat surface that has been dusted with oat flour, roll out the dough to about ½ inch thick. Using 3 ½ inch dough cutter (a water glass works well here) cut the dough and place on a cookie sheet sprayed with a bit of cooking spray. Cover and allow to double in size. Bake for 20 – 25 minutes, this recipe will make about 12 buns.

Calorie Count:	
Olive Oil –	120
Gluten –	360
Oat Flour –	624
Honey –	60
Total:	1164
Per Roll:	97.0
Carbohydrates Count:	
Olive Oil –	0
Gluten –	18
Oat Flour –	96
Honey –	15
Total:	129
Per Roll:	10.8

Bagels

As good as the bagel from the local deli, use it from breakfast or for sandwiches.

1 ¼ of cups water
1 teaspoon salt
3/4 cup vital wheat gluten
2 cups oat flour
1 tablespoon honey
1 tablespoon yeast

1 gallon boiling water

1 egg substitute mixed with 1 teaspoon cold water

Heat oven to warm, when it reaches this temperature shut off oven. Add ingredients in order to bread machine, run machine in dough mode and run it to mix and knead. When the machine switches to raise mode remove the dough. Cut the dough into quarters and then eights. Shape each piece into a flattened ball; put your finger through the middle of each ball and stretch it to form a wide hole, place on a cookie sheet, repeat with remaining dough. Place uncovered into the oven for 15 minutes, (start your water to boiling) remove from the oven. Set the oven to 425 degrees. Put each bagel into boiling water for about 1 minute on each side (don't crowd them, a couple at a time will do). Remove with a slotted spoon to a rack and allow to cool for a few minutes. Brush the bagels with the egg mixture and bake in the oven for 20 minutes; remove to the racks to cool. This recipe will make 8 bagels.

Calorie Count:	
Gluten –	360
Oat Flour –	624
Honey –	60
Egg substitute –	30
Total:	1074
Per Bagel:	134.3
Carbohydrates Count:	
Gluten –	18
Oat Flour –	96
Honey –	15
Egg substitute –	1
Total:	130
Per Bagel:	16.3

Soft Pretzels

For a treat spread a bit of good quality brown mustard on one of these and enjoy!

1 cup water
2 tablespoons Spread
1 teaspoon salt
2 cups oat flour
½ cup vital wheat gluten

1 gallon water
4 tablespoons baking soda

2 teaspoons kosher salt

Heat oven to warm, when it reaches this temperature shut off oven. Add ingredients in order to bread machine run machine in dough mode and run it to mix and knead. When the machine switches to raise mode remove the dough. Roll into a rope about 24 inches long and cut into 2 inch slices. Roll each slice into a rope 12 – 15 inches long, shape into pretzel and place on a cookie sheet, repeat with each slice. Allow to rise for 1 hour. Pre-heat the oven to 425 degrees. Add the soda to the gallon of water and bring to a light boil. Put a pretzel into the boiling water for about 1 minute, remove to a cooling rack and sprinkle with a couple of pinches of kosher salt, repeat with the remaining pretzels. Place the pretzel on a cookie sheet (or two) that is sprayed with a bit of cooking spray. Bake for 12 minutes and remove to rake to cool. This recipe will makes 12 pretzels.

Calorie Count:	
Gluten –	240
Oat Flour –	624
Spread–	90
Total:	954
Per Pretzel:	79.5
Carbohydrates Count:	
Gluten –	12
Oat Flour –	96
Spread –	0
Total:	108
Per Bagel:	9.0

Pizza dough

Be careful of the topping you put on this, they can add up quickly in the calorie and carbohydrate department, keep it simple.

1 cup water
1 tablespoon Spread
1 teaspoon salt
2 cups oat flour
¾ cup vital wheat gluten
1 tablespoon honey
1 tablespoon yeast

Add ingredients to bread machine in order listed. Run machine on quick bread mode, when kneaded unplug machine and allow to rise in the machine. When double in size and remove from bread machine and punch down. Roll into a large thin circle and prepare as any other pizza. Recipe makes 1 16 inch crust, cut pizza into 16 slices for serving.

Calorie Count:	
Gluten –	360
Oat Flour –	624
Honey –	60
Spread –	45
Total:	1089
Per Slice:	68.1
Carbohydrates Count:	
Gluten –	18
Oat Flour –	96
Honey –	15
Spread –	0
Total:	129
Per Slice:	8.1

Beefy pinwheels

Freeze these for later use; they make a quick meal when you're on the go.

1 recipe of bread dough (add 1 heaping teaspoon of beef base to the water when preparing do not add the salt)
1/2 cup chopped green pepper
1/2 cup finely chopped onion

Pre-heat the oven to 400 degrees, roll dough into a rectangle about 15 inches long and 6 inches wide, press onion and green pepper into flattened dough. Roll up in to a tight jell roll and slice into 12 roughly equal portions. Place on cookie sheet that has been sprayed with a bit of cooking spray and allow to rize until doubled. Bake for 10 - 15 minutes or until golden brown. Serve hot as is or with a bit of beef gravy. This recipe makes about 12 rolls

Calorie Count:	
Bread –	1119
Beef Base –	45
Onion –	30
Green Pepper –	24
Total:	1218
Per roll:	101.5
Carbohydrates Count:	
Bread –	130
Beef Base –	1
Onion –	8.9
Green Pepper –	2.5
Total:	142.4
Per roll:	11.9

Pizza rolls

An alternative to boring flat pizza, add some cooked Italian sausage, but don't forget to adjust the calorie and carbohydrate count.

1 recipe of bread dough
1/4 cup pizza sauce
1/3 cup Weight Watchers shredded Mozzarella cheese

Pre-heat oven to 400 degrees, roll dough into a rectangle about 15 inches long and 6 inches wide, paint on the pizza sauce and sprinkle the cheese evenly over the dough. Roll up tightly in a jell roll and slice into 12 roughly equal portions. Place on cookie sheets that have been sprayed with a bit of cooking spray and allow to rise until doubled. Bake for 10 - 15 minutes or until golden brown. Serve hot as is or with a bit of warm pizza sauce. This recipe makes 12 rolls.

Calorie Count:	
Bread –	1119
Pizza sauce –	60
Cheese –	106.7
Total:	1285.7
Per roll:	107.1
Carbohydrates Count:	
Bread –	130
Pizza sauce –	8
Cheese –	1.3
Total:	139.3
Per Roll:	11.6

Puff Pastry

You wouldn't think that this was even possible, yet it works well and is very tasty.

1 cups water
1 teaspoon salt
3/4 cup vital wheat gluten
2 cups oat flour
1 tablespoon honey
2 tablespoon yeast
3 tablespoons Spread

Combine 1 cup water, salt, oat flour, wheat gluten, honey and yeast in your bread machine, run on quick setting but remove after 8 minutes (kneading too long can cause the dough to be tough). Dust your working surface with a bit of oat flour and roll dough to about 12 inches square. Spread the Spread on the surface of the dough, fold in thirds and roll out. At this point wrap dough and place in freezer for 15 minutes, remove roll out and fold and replace in freezer, repeat 5 more times. Dough is now ready for a various recipes.

Calorie Count:	
Spread –	135
Gluten –	360
Oat Flour –	624
Honey –	60
Total:	1179

Carbohydrates Count:	
Gluten –	18
Oat Flour –	96
Honey –	15
Spread –	0
Total:	129

Croissants

1 recipe Puffed Pastry
1 egg substitute beaten with 1 teaspoon of cold water

Pre-heat the oven to 450 degrees. Spray a cookie sheet lightly with cooking spray. On the last roll out of the puff pastry roll it out to a rectangle about 18 inches long by 10 inches wide. With a very sharp knife cut the dough width wise in half. You will now have two sheets about 18 by 5, cut each into a triangles about 2 and ½ inches at the base, roll each into a crescent shape and place on cookie sheet, brush with the egg water mixture, cover and let rise for 30 – 45 minutes. Bake for 12 – 15 minutes. This recipe will makes 14 rolls.

Calorie Count:	
Puffed Pastry –	1179
Egg substitute –	30
Total:	1209
Per Croissants:	86.4
Carbohydrates Count:	
Puffed Pastry –	141
Egg substitute –	2
Total:	143
Per Croissants:	10.2

Puff Biscuits

You may want to cut these in squares with a very sharp knife, rather than using the biscuit cutter, re-rolling the scraps works, but cut square produced more biscuits and they will puff better.

1 recipe Puffed Pastry
1 egg substitute beaten with 1/2 teaspoon of cold water

Pre-heat the oven to 400 degrees. Spray a cookie sheet lightly with cooking spray. On the last roll out of the puff pastry roll it out to a rectangle about 1 half of an inch thick. Cut with a 2 ½ inch biscuit cutter and place on cookie sheet gather the scraps and re-roll (these will puff in odd configurations, but they will puff), brush with the egg water mixture, cover and let rise for 30 – 45 minutes. Bake for 12 – 15 minutes. This recipe will makes about 12 biscuits.

Calorie Count:	
Puffed Pastry –	1179
Egg substitute –	30
Total:	1209
Per Biscuits:	100.8
Carbohydrates Count:	
Puffed Pastry –	129
Egg substitute –	1
Total:	130
Per Biscuits:	10.8

English Muffins

A bit denser than the Standard English muffin but with many nooks and crannies and delicious

1 ½ of cup water
1 tablespoon fat free dry milk
1 tablespoon Honey
1 tablespoon Spread
2 cups oat flour
¾ cup vital gluten
1/2 teaspoon salt
1 tablespoon baking powder
2 tablespoons yeast

Place the ingredients in order in your bread machine and run in quick mode through the knead cycle. Remove and roll out to about ½ inch thick, the dough will be sticky. Cut into 3 inch or so round loafs. Place on a cookie sheet dusted with oat flour and allow to rise until double in height. Heat a griddle to a high medium and place the risen muffins on the griddle (a few at a time), cook for 10 – 15 minutes, flip and cook the other side for about the same amount of time, move to a rack repeat with the remaining muffins allow to cooling completely, brushing off the oat flour that has adhered to both sides. This recipe will make about 18, 3 inch diameter muffins.

Calorie Count:	
Gluten –	360
Oat Flour –	624
Honey –	60
Spread –	45
Dry Milk –	15
Baking powder –	6
Total:	1110
Per muffin:	61.7
Carbohydrates Count:	
Gluten –	18
Oat Flour –	96
Honey –	15
Spread –	0
Dry Milk –	2.25
Baking Powder –	3.8
Total:	135.05
Per muffin:	7.5

Sweets

I don't know about you, but for me sweets have always been one of the downfalls when trying to lose weight (next to bread). Have a candy bar, or a piece of cake and the next day your weight will probably not be significantly different than your weight on the previous day, do that every day and the calories and carbohydrates add up and you will gain weight. That single instance of sweet indulgence seems to somehow embolden me and I generally have to take the situation in hand to break the cycle. Its better (way better) to not start the cycle at all, and that is what this chapter is about, these recipes help me not take that first bit of Milky Way or Little Debby or chocolate covered doughnut, etc. etc.

A stack of cinnamon rolls (recipe number 1) breakfast fair supreme

Basic Sweet Dough

This dough will be used as the base for a number of recipes; the use of Splenda® reduces the carbohydrates, unlike what you read in the press, it does not eliminate them.

1 cups water
¼ cup egg substitute
1 tablespoon Spread
1 teaspoon salt
1 tablespoon honey
1 cup Splenda®
3/4 cup vital wheat gluten
2 cups oat flour
2 tablespoon yeast

Add ingredients in order listed to bread machine, run machine in quick mode, run it to mix and knead. When the machine switches to raise mode remove the dough and use for recipes. The dough should be soft and sticky.

Calorie Count:	
Egg substitute –	30
Spread –	45
Gluten –	360
Oat Flour –	624
Honey –	60
Splenda® –	96
Total:	1215
Carbohydrates Count:	
Gluten –	18
Oat Flour –	96
Honey –	15
Splenda® –	24
Egg substitute –	1
Spread –	0
Total:	154

Sweet Puff Pastry

Sweeter pastry for sweeter results

1 cups water
1 tablespoon honey
1 teaspoon salt
½ cup Splenda®
3/4 cup vital wheat gluten
2 cups oat flour
2 tablespoon yeast
3 tablespoons spread

Prepare as you would puff pastry, add the Splenda® to the dough after the salt, but before the gluten and oat flour, it will dissolve in water.

Calorie Count:	
Spread –	135
Splenda® –	48
Gluten –	360
Oat Flour –	624
Honey –	60
Total:	1227
Carbohydrates Count:	
Gluten –	18
Oat Flour –	96
Honey –	15
Splenda® –	12
Spread –	0
Total:	141

Raised Cinnamon Doughnuts

Be sure to have the oil at temperature and do not prick the surface of the doughnut, the idea is to crisp the outside and not let the oil to penetrate.

1 recipe of Basic sweet dough
2 tablespoons of cinnamon
1 teaspoon Allspice
Vegetable oil for frying

Add the cinnamon and Allspice to the dough just after the oat flour, make as usual. Gently roll dough 1/2-inch thick with floured rolling pin on a surface dusted with oat flour. Cut with doughnut cutter dipped into oat flour. Cover and let rise until double, 30-40 minutes. In the mean time heat vegetable oil in deep fat fryer to 375 degrees slide doughnuts into hot oil with wide spatula. Turn doughnuts as they rise to the surface. Fry until golden brown, about 1 minute on each side. Remove carefully from oil (do not prick surface); place on a cooling rack with a padding of paper towels under to catch the drippings oil. This recipe will makes about 18 doughnuts.

Calorie Count:	
Sweet Dough –	1179
Cinnamon –	34
Allspice –	10
Total:	1223
Per Doughnut:	67.9
Carbohydrates Count:	
Sweet Dough –	141
Cinnamon –	11
Allspice –	2
Total:	154
Per Doughnut:	8.6

Cake Doughnuts

As good a doughnut as you will find in any shop

½ cup Egg substitute
2 tablespoons Spread
2/3 cup Yogurt
1 teaspoon Allspice
1 cup Splenda®
2 ½ cups oat flour, sifted
¾ cup vital gluten, sifted
2 tablespoons baking powder
2 tablespoons of cinnamon

Vegetable oil for frying

Combine all dry ingredients in order in which are listed, combine the wet ingredients and mix with a hand mixture till will combine. Add dry ingredients to the wet and mix, remove to flat surface and knead for about 3 minutes, place in a bowl and refrigerate for at least 2 hours, covered. Remove to your dusted flat surface and roll out to about ½ inch thickness cut with a doughnut cutter. Re-combine the scraps and cut additional doughnuts.   Heat vegetable oil in deep fat fryer to 375 degrees. Slide doughnuts into hot oil with wide spatula. Turn doughnuts as they rise to the surface. Fry until golden brown, about 1 minute on each side. Remove carefully from oil (do not prick surface). Recipe will makes about 18 doughnuts.

Calorie Count:	
Egg substitute –	60
Spread –	90
Gluten –	360
Oat Flour –	780
Yogurt –	73.26
Splenda® –	96
Cinnamon –	34
Allspice –	10
Baking Powder –	12
Total:	1515.26
Per Doughnut:	84.2
Carbohydrates Count:	
Egg substitute –	2
Spread–	0
Gluten –	18
Oat Flour –	120
Yogurt –	13.99
Splenda® –	24
Cinnamon –	11
Allspice –	2
Baking Powder –	7.6
Total:	198.59
Per Doughnut:	11.0

Cinnamon Rolls #1

They should be relegated to treat status, simply because it's difficult to eat just one.

1 recipe of sweet dough
¼ cup Splenda®
¼ cup Splenda brown sugar Blend®
2 tablespoons cinnamon

Pre-heat your oven to 375 degrees, mix the Splenda®, Splenda brown sugar blend® and cinnamon set aside. Roll out the bread dough into a rectangle about 20 inches long and 6 inches wide, spray the surface with a bit of cooking spray and sprinkle the Splenda® mixture over the dough and press in. Roll up jelly roll fashion (from the wide side) and slice with a very sharp knife into 20 roughly equal portions, place into a 9 x 12 cake pan (that has been sprayed lightly with cooking spray), they should be just touching. Allow to rise till double then bake for 30 minutes. This recipe will make 20 rolls.

Calorie Count:	
Sweet Dough –	1215
Cinnamon –	34
Splenda Brown Sugar Blend® –	240
Splenda® –	24
Total:	1513
Pre roll:	75.65
Carbohydrates Count:	
Sweet Dough –	154
Cinnamon –	11
Splenda Brown Sugar Blend® –	48
Splenda® –	6
Total:	219
Pre roll:	10.95

Cinnamon Rolls #2

Slightly less in the carbohydrate count and slightly more in the calorie count than cinnamon roll recipe #1, but equal in taste.

1 Recipe of Sweet Puff Pastry
¼ cup Splenda®
¼ cup Splenda brown sugar Blend®
2 tablespoons cinnamon
1 tablespoon of Spread

Pre-heat oven to 350 degrees. Mix the Splenda®'s and cinnamon in a small bowl and set aside. Prepare the puff pastry as directed elsewhere; roll out the dough into a rectangle about 20 inches wide by 8 inches high. Evenly coat the surface of the dough with the Spread and sprinkle the Splenda® mixture evenly over the dough. Roll this up jelly roll fashion and seal the edge with a little water. Cut with a very sharp knife into 20 equal rolls and place on non-stick cookie sheets that have been sprayed lightly with cooking spray. Cover and allow rising till triple in size. If you like spray the tops of the rolls very lightly with a butter flavored cooking spray and sprinkle with a pinch of granulated sugar, but adjust the calorie and carbohydrate count accordingly. Bake for 15 – 20 minutes, this recipe makes about 20 rolls.

Calorie Count:	
Puff Pastry –	1179
Cinnamon –	34
Splenda Brown Sugar Blend® –	240
Splenda® –	24
Spread –	45
Total:	1522
Pre roll:	76.1
Carbohydrates Count:	
Puff Pastry –	141
Cinnamon –	11
Splenda Brown Sugar Blend® –	48
Splenda® –	6
Spread –	0
Total:	206
Pre roll:	10.3

Basic vanilla cake

½ cup vital wheat gluten
1½ cups oat flour
1 cup Splenda®
2 tablespoons baking powder
1/2 cup egg substitute
1 cup Yogurt

Pre-heat the oven to 375 degrees. Sift together all of the dry ingredients, make a well in the middle of this mixture and place into it the wet ingredients. Mix very well. Spray an 8 inch square baking pan (I prefer glass) with a cooking spray and pour mixture into baking dish and level. Bake for 30 minutes, test for doneness by inserting a toothpick, if it comes out clean the cake is done. Cut the cake into 12 equal size slices. If you wish top each slice with a teaspoon of yogurt or oat milk whipped cream, but add in the extra calories and carbohydrates.

Calorie Count:	
Egg substitute –	60
Gluten –	240
Oat Flour –	468
Yogurt –	110
Splenda® –	96
Baking Powder –	12
Total:	986
Per slice:	82.2
Carbohydrates Count:	
Egg substitute –	2
Gluten –	12
Oat Flour –	72
Yogurt –	21
Splenda® –	24
Baking Powder –	7.6
Total:	138.6
Per Slice:	11.6

Blueberry Coffee cake

My absolute favorite coffee cake recipe from before my diet days, converted to keep me from consuming the original.

¼ cup egg substitute
1 cup milk (made from 1/3 cup of none fat dried milk)
1/2 cup Yogurt
3/4 cup Splenda®
1 cup oat flour
1/2 cup gluten
2 tablespoons of baking power
1 heaping cup blueberries

Pre-heat oven to 375 degrees, spray an 8 x 8 inch pan with cooking spray. Mix the dried milk with enough water to equal 1 cup. Then combine the egg substitute, milk, yogurt and Splenda® Wisk until well mixed. Sift oat flour; gluten and baking powder into liquid mixture and mix until just combined add blueberries and lightly mix till incorporated. Put into pan and spread out until evenly bake for 35 minutes. Cut into 12 equal servings, serve warm.

Calorie Count:	
Egg substitute –	60
Milk –	79.95
Yogurt –	55
Oat flour –	312
Gluten –	240
Blueberries –	79
Splenda® –	72
Baking Powder –	12
Total	909.95
Per slice:	75.8
Carbohydrates Count:	
Egg substitute –	2
Gluten –	12
Oat Flour –	48
Yogurt –	10.5
Splenda® –	18
Baking Powder –	7.6
Blueberries –	14.7
Milk –	11.99
Total·	124.79
Per slice:	10.4

Spice Cake

The combination of cinnamon, allspice and cloves give this cake a classic taste.

1 1/2 cups yogurt
1/2 cup egg substitute
1 cup milk (made from 1/3 cup of none fat dried milk)
1 1/2 cup oat flour
1/2 cup gluten
3/4 cups Splenda®
2 tablespoons baking powder
2 tablespoons cinnamon
1 teaspoon allspice
1 teaspoon grounds cloves

Pre-heat your oven to 350 degrees. Mix the dried milk with sufficient water to equal 1 cup. Mix the yogurt, egg substitute and milk. Sift in the dry materials, and mix till completely mixed. Spoon the mixture into an 8x8 cake pan that has been sprayed lightly with a cooking spray, bake for about 35 minutes. Cut into 12 equal size pieces. Top each slice with a teaspoon of vanilla yogurt, or an equal amount of oat milk whipped cream.

Calorie Count:	
Yogurt –	165
Egg substitute –	60
Oat flour –	468
Gluten –	240
Splenda® –	72
Milk –	79.95
Baking powder –	12
Cinnamon –	34
Allspice –	10
Cloves –	7
Total:	1147.95
Pre slice:	95.66
Carbohydrates Count:	
Egg substitute –	2
Gluten –	12
Oat Flour –	72
Yogurt –	31.5
Splenda® –	18
Baking Powder –	7.6
Milk –	11.99
Cinnamon –	11
Allspice –	2
Cloves –	1.3
Total:	169.39
Pre slice:	14.1

Cake Brownies

Brownies have always been one of my weaknesses; just for fun compare the calories and carbohydrates in this recipe to a regular one.

1 cup egg substitute
2/3 cup Yogurt
2 cups Splenda®
1/2 cup Cocoa powder
3/4 cup oat flour
1/4 cup vital wheat gluten
2 tablespoons baking powder

Pre-heat oven to 350 degrees, spray an 8x8 baking pan with cooking spray. Place the first 3 ingredients in a large bowl and whisk until well mixed. Sift in the last 4 ingredients and mixed, Spoon into baking dish and bake for about 35 minutes, or until a toothpick comes out clean. Cut into 12 equal size pieces. The cake may be frosted with frosting recipe found elsewhere in the book, factor in the calories and carbohydrates.

.

Calorie Count:	
Egg substitute –	120
Yogurt –	73.26
Oat flour –	234
Gluten –	120
Cocoa powder –	160
Splenda® –	192
Baking powder –	12
Total	911.26
Per slice:	75.9
Carbohydrates Count:	
Egg substitute –	4
Yogurt –	13.99
Splenda® –	48
Gluten –	6
Oat Flour –	36
Baking Powder –	7.6
Cocoa powder –	16
Total	131.586
Per slice:	11.0

Apple Cake

Try this with granny smith apples; a touch of cinnamon will add an additional dimension to this cake, and not a lot of extra calories and carbohydrates. .

¼ cup Yogurt
½ cup Splenda®
¾ cup egg substitute
3 medium apples, peeled, cored and diced
1 cup oat flour
1/4 cup gluten
2 tablespoons baking powder

Pre-heat your oven to 350 degrees, combine the yogurt, Splenda® and egg substitute and mix until well incorporated, sift in the dry ingredients and mix. Stir in the diced apples; pour the mixture into an 8x8 inch pan that has been sprayed with a bit of cooking spray. Bake for 30 minutes or until a toothpick comes out clean. Cool and cut into 12 squares. Top with yogurt at serving time, add in the calories and carbohydrates if you opt for this option.

Calorie Count:	
Yogurt –	55
Splenda® –	48
Egg substitute –	90
Gluten –	120
Oat flour –	312
Baking powder –	12
Apples –	183
Total	820
Per slice:	68.3
Carbohydrates Count:	
Yogurt –	10.5
Splenda® –	12
Egg substitute –	3
Gluten –	6
Oat Flour –	48
Baking Powder –	7.6
Apples –	43.89
Total	130.99
Per slice:	10.9

Basic Cupcakes

These will start you on the cupcake trains; just watch what you put on them as it can add up quickly.

1 cup Splenda®
¾ cup egg substitute
¼ cup egg white powder
¼ teaspoon cream of tartar
¾ cup cold water
3/4 cup oat flour
1/4 cup gluten
1 tablespoon baking powder
1 teaspoon vanilla

Pre-heat your oven to 350 degrees, clean and dry 6 coffee cups (NOT PLASTIC!). Beat together the egg white powder, cream of tartar and ¾ cup of cold water until stiff. Combine the Splenda®, vanilla and egg substitute and beat until thickened, sift in the oat flour, gluten and baking powder, add 1/3 of the egg whites and mix lightly, add another 1/3 of the egg whites and fold in, and the last 1/3 and fold in. Divide the mixture between the 6 coffee cups, bake for 30 minutes. Cool completely before attempting to remove from the coffee cups, do so by running a thin sharp knife between the cup and cake to loosen.

Calorie Count:	
Oat flour –	234
Gluten –	120
Egg Substitute –	90
Egg whites –	72
Splenda® –	96
Baking powder–	6
Vanilla –	36
Cream of tartar –	2
Total	656
Per cup cake:	109.3
Carbohydrates Count:	
Oat flour –	36
Gluten –	6
Egg Substitute –	3
Egg whites –	0
Splenda® –	24
Baking powder–	3.8
Vanilla –	1.5
Cream of tartar –	0.5
Total	74.76
Per cup cake:	12.5

Rusk

A very old recipe, pre dates the twice baked biscuit that carries that name today.

2 cups oat flour
3/4 cup gluten
1 tablespoon baking soda
1 teaspoon nutmeg
1 tablespoon cinnamon
½ teaspoon cloves
1 cup Splenda®
½ cup Yogurt
¼ cup egg substitute
1 ½ cups of water (with 1 teaspoon of white vinegar mixed in)

Pre-heat your oven to 350 degrees, sift together all of the dry ingredients, and add yogurt, water and the egg substitute. Stir until well mixed then pour into an 8x8 baking pan that has been sprayed with a bit of cooking spray, do this quickly. Bake for 45 minutes to 1 hour or until a toothpick inserted into the center comes out clean, cool and cut into 12 equal squares.

Calorie Count:	
Gluten –	360
Oat Flour –	624
Baking Soda –	0
Nutmeg –	37
Cinnamon –	17
Cloves –	3.5
Splenda® –	96
Egg substitute –	30
Yogurt –	55
Total	1222.5
Per slice:	101.9

Carbohydrates Count:	
Gluten –	18
Oat Flour –	96
Baking Soda –	0
Nutmeg –	3.5
Cinnamon –	5.5
Cloves –	0.65
Splenda® –	24
Egg substitute –	1
Yogurt –	10.5
Total	159.15
Per slice:	13.3

Yogurt Cinnamon Buns

Because of the higher calorie and carbohydrate count of these rolls I make them only as a treat, and freeze the leftovers for later breakfasts, you can also slice them thinner and decrease the counts.

1/4 cup Splenda brown sugar Blend®
2 tablespoons of Cinnamon
2 cups oat flour
3/4 cup gluten
2 tablespoons baking powder
1 cup Yogurt
1/4 cup Splenda®

Pre-heat oven to 450 degrees; mix Splenda® brown sugar Blend® and Cinnamon set aside. Place yogurt and the ¼ cup of Splenda® in a bowl, Sift in the oat flour, gluten and baking powder mix to just incorporate. Spread a bit of oat flout on a flat surface and dump the mixture onto it. Knead 10 or so time till combined and smooth. Roll into a rectangle about 6 inches by 12 inches spray with a bit of cooking spray and spread the brown sugar mixture on top, lightly press it in. Carefully roll up jelly roll fashion and cut into 8 equal slices, place on a cookie sheet bake for about 20 minutes. .

Calorie Count:	
Splenda Brown Sugar Blend® –	240
Cinnamon –	34
Gluten –	360
Oat Flour –	624
Baking Powder –	12
Yogurt –	110
Splenda® –	24
Total	1404
Per bun:	175.5
Carbohydrates Count:	
Splenda Brown Sugar Blend® –	48
Cinnamon –	11
Gluten –	18
Oat Flour –	96
Baking Powder –	7.6
Yogurt –	21
Splenda® –	6
Total	207.6
Per bun:	26.0

Honey Crackers

Use these are replacements for graham crackers, crumbled and combined with a bit of melted Spread might even work as a taste pie crust.

1 cup water
1/4 cup Yogurt
1 tablespoon honey
1 tablespoon vanilla
¼ cup egg substitute
1 teaspoons salt
2 ½ - 3 cups all oat flour
1/2 cup vital wheat gluten
1 teaspoon baking soda
1 tablespoon cinnamon
1/3 cup Splenda®
1/8 cup Splenda brown sugar Blend®

Add ingredients in order listed to bread machine, run machine in dough mode if the mixture looks too thin at a bit more oat flour. When the machine switches to raise mode remove the dough and place in a zip lock bag, put in refrigerator for at least 1 hour. Remove and cut into quarters, return 3 of the quarters to the refrigerator. Pre-heat the oven to 350 degrees. Roll out the dough on a lightly dusted work surface (dusted with oat flour) as thin as possible. Cut into 2 by 2 inch squares, with a fork puncher the dough repeatedly, place on a non-stick cookie sheet, sprayed with a bit of cooking spray. Bake for 9 minutes, flip and bake for another 9 minutes. Remove to a wire rake to cool. Repeat with the remaining dough. This will make about 60 crackers.

Calorie Count:	
Yogurt –	27.5
Honey –	60
Vanilla –	36
Egg substitute –	30
Oat Flour –	780
Gluten –	240
Baking Soda –	0
Cinnamon –	17
Splenda® –	31.97
Splenda Brown Sugar Blend® –	120
Total	1342.47
Per Cracker:	22.4
Carbohydrates Count:	
Yogurt –	5.25
Honey –	15
Vanilla –	1.5
Egg substitute –	1
Gluten –	12
Oat Flour –	120
Baking Soda –	0
Cinnamon –	5.5
Splenda® –	7.992
Splenda Brown Sugar Blend® –	24
Total	192.24
Per Cracker:	3.2

Oatmeal Cookies

One of my favorite oat delivery systems

1 cup oat flour
1/2 cup gluten
1 tablespoon baking powder
2/3 cup Splenda®
1 tablespoon cinnamon

1 1/2 cup old fashioned oats

¼ cup egg substitute
3/4 cup yogurt

Pre-heat the oven to 350 degrees. Sift together oat flour, gluten and baking powder. Add the oats, Splenda® and cinnamon mix until well combined. Mix together the egg substitute and yogurt add to the dry ingredients and mix well. Cover and place in the refrigerator for 2 or 3 hours. Remove and place a heaping tablespoon on a cookie sheet that has been sprayed with a non-fat cooking spray. With a fork (dipped lightly in oat flour) press the cookies flat repeat with the rest of the dough. Bake for 15 minutes. Makes about 24 cookies

Calorie Count:	
Oat Flour –	312
Gluten –	240
Baking Soda –	0
Splenda® –	63.94
Cinnamon –	17
Oats –	249
Egg substitute –	30
Yogurt –	82.5
Total	994.44
Per Cookie:	41.4
Carbohydrates Count:	
Oat Flour –	48
Gluten –	12
Baking Soda –	0
Splenda® –	15.98
Cinnamon –	5.5
Oats –	36.15
Egg substitute –	1
Yogurt –	15.75
Total	134.38
Per Cookie:	5.6

Chocolate Chip Cookies

Life in not complete without at least a little chocolate

1 cup Splenda®
1/8 cup Splenda Brown Sugar Blend®
2 tablespoon Spread
¼ cup egg substitute
½ cup Yogurt
1 cup oat flour
1/2 cup vital gluten
1 tablespoon baking powder
3 oz. of mini chocolate chips

Pre-heat the oven to 350 degrees. In a large bowl place the egg substitute, Spread, Splenda®, Splenda Brown Sugar Blend® and the yogurt, mix with a hand mixer till completely incorporated. Sift in the oat flour, gluten and baking powder and mix well (adjust with a little extra oat flour if to thin, or extra yogurt if too thick), add the chocolate chip and mixed until well distributed. Spoon 1 heaping tablespoon of the mixture onto a non-stick cookie sheet, use a fork (dipped in water) to flatten the cookie repeat with remaining dough, bake for 13 – 15 minutes remove from the oven to a cooling rack. Recipe will make about 22 cookies.

Calorie Count:	
Splenda® –	96
Splenda Brown Sugar Blend® –	120
Spread –	90
Egg substitute –	30
Yogurt –	55
Oat Flour –	312
Gluten –	240
Baking Powder –	6
Chocolate chips –	425
Total	1374
Per Cookie:	62.5
Carbohydrates Count:	
Splenda® –	24
Splenda Brown Sugar Blend® –	24
Spread –	0
Egg substitute –	1
Yogurt –	10.5
Oat Flour –	48
Gluten –	12
Baking Powder –	3.8
Chocolate chips –	53.9
Total	177.2
Per Cookie:	8.1

Sugarless Cookies

Good at Christmas, rolled out and cut into festive shapes.

1 cup Splenda®
2 tablespoon Spread
¼ cup egg substitute
½ cup Yogurt
1 ½ cup of oat flour
1/2 cup vital gluten
1 tablespoon baking powder

Pre-heat the oven to 375 degrees. In a large bowl place the egg substitute, Spread, Splenda®, and the yogurt, mix with a hand mixer till completely incorporated. Sift in the oat flour, gluten and baking powder and hand mix well with a stout spoon. Sprinkle a bit of oat flour on your working surface and remove the mixture to this, roll the dough to a log about 10 inches long, wrap in aluminum foil, refrigerate for at least 2 hours (overnight is better). Slice in 3/16 inch slices and place on a non-stick cookie sheet. Bake for 8 - 10 minutes remove from the oven to a cooling rack. Recipe will make about 24 cookies.

Calorie Count:	
Splenda® –	96
Spread –	90
Egg substitute –	30
Yogurt –	55
Oat Flour –	468
Gluten –	240
Baking Powder –	6
Total	985
Per Cookie:	41.0
Carbohydrates Count:	
Splenda® –	24
Spread –	0
Egg substitute –	1
Yogurt –	10.5
Oat Flour –	72
Gluten –	12
Baking Powder –	3.8
Total	123.3
Per Cookie:	5.1

Yogurt pie crust

3/4 cups oat flour
1/4 cup gluten
1/2 teaspoon salt
1/4 cup Splenda®
2 tablespoons Spread
1 tablespoon yogurt
2 to 4 tablespoons cold water

Sift together oat flour, gluten and salt. Add Spread and yogurt cut into flour using a pastry blender or fork (I prefer a simple fork for this process). Add cold water and mix until flour is moistened and has formed a dough, chill for at least 1 hour (overnight is better). Roll out on board floured with oat flour. This recipe will makes 1 8 or 9-inch crusts.

Calorie Count:	
Oat Flour –	234
Gluten –	120
Splenda® –	24
Spread –	90
Yogurt –	6.88
Total	474.88
Carbohydrates Count:	
Oat Flour –	36
Gluten –	6
Splenda® –	6
Spread –	0
Yogurt –	1.31
Total	49.31

Banana Cream pie

To drastically lower the calorie and carbohydrate count us oat milk cooking instead of instant milk.

1 recipe yogurt pie single crust (baked)
1 medium bananas, peeled and thinly sliced
1 box Jell-O® Sugar free instant banana cream pie filling
2/3 cup instant dried milk

Mix the instant milk with enough water to make 2 cups. Into the cooled pie crust place the sliced bananas. Follow the recipe on the box for mixing the Jell-O for pie filling, using the instant milk, pour over the banana and refrigerate until firm. Slice into 8 equal servings. Top each slice with a teaspoon of yogurt or oat milk whipped cream.

Calorie Count:	
Yogurt pie crust –	474.88
Banana –	105
Pie filling –	100
Fat free dry milk –	159.9
Total	839.78
Per Slice:	105.0
Carbohydrates Count:	
Yogurt pie crust –	49.3
Banana –	26.9
Pie filling –	24
Fat free dry milk –	23.99
Total	124.19
Per Slice:	15.5

Breakfast pie

Probably my favorite breakfast

1 recipe yogurt pie crust
Reduce sugar raspberry jam
1 tablespoon egg substitute mixed with 1
tablespoon water

Pre-heat your oven to 450 degrees, divide the dough into two equal portions, roll each out into a rectangle about 12 inches wide and 24 inches long, cut them into 6 equal rectangles. Place a teaspoon of jam on 6 of the rectangles cover with the other 6 rectangles first having run a little water around the parameter of the dough and seal the edges with a fork making sure that they are well sealed. With a fork puncher the top layer of the pastry a number of times do not puncher all the way through, place them on a non-stick cookie sheet. Paint the surface with a bit of egg substitute mixture. Bake for 10 – 15 minutes or until browned, serve cold or put into a toaster for a few minutes to reheat.

Calorie Count:	
Yogurt pie crust –	474.9
Egg substitute –	7.5
Raspberry jam –	150
Total	632.4
Per Slice:	105.4
Carbohydrates Count:	
Yogurt pie crust –	49.3
Egg substitute –	0.5
Raspberry jam –	36
Total	85.8
Per Slice:	14.3

Kringle

A tribute to my Danish roots, on my mother's side.

1 recipe sweet puff pastry
1 tablespoon Spread
¼ cup Splenda®
¼ cup Splenda Brown Sugar Blend®
2 tablespoons cinnamon
1 egg substitute beaten with 1 teaspoon cold water

Pre-heat the oven to 450 degrees. Spray a cookie sheet lightly with cooking spray. Prepare puff pastry in the normal fashion. On the last roll out of the puff pastry roll it out to a rectangle about 20 inches long by 10 inches wide. Combine the Splenda®, Splenda Brown Sugar Blend® and cinnamon. Thinly spread the tablespoon of Spread on the half of the dough nearest to you, sprinkle on the Splenda®, brown sugar mixture over the spread. Paint the edge of the dough with a bit of the egg mixture and fold the section that's not covered with mixture over the section that is covered, seal the edges. Position on the cookie sheet and allow to rise for 15 minutes. Paint the surface with the egg mixture, bake for 12 – 15 minutes, and slip onto a cooling rake. Cut into 20 1 inch sections.

Calorie Count:	
Puff Pastry –	1179
Spread –	45
Splenda® –	24
Splenda Brown Sugar Blend® –	240
Cinnamon –	34
Egg substitute –	30
Total	1552
Per Slice:	77.6
Carbohydrates Count:	
Puff Pastry –	141
Spread–	0
Splenda® –	24
Splenda Brown Sugar Blend® –	48
Cinnamon –	11
Egg substitute –	1
Total	225
Per Slice:	11.3

Butterscotch Pie

Oat milk cooking may be used as a substitute for the instant milk mixture.

1 recipe yogurt pie single crust (baked)
1 box Jell-O® Sugar free instant butterscotch pie filling
2/3 cup instant dried milk

Mix the instant milk with enough water to make 2 cups. Follow the recipe on the box for mixing the Jell-O for pie filling, pour into pre-baked pie crust and refrigerate until firm. Slice into 8 equal servings. A topping of yogurt oat milk whipped cream is excellent on this pie.

Calorie Count:	
Yogurt pie crust –	474.88
Pie filling –	100
Fat free dry milk –	159.9
Total	734.78
Per Slice:	91.8
Carbohydrates Count:	
Yogurt pie crust –	49.31
Pie filling –	24
Fat free dry milk –	23.99
Total	97.30
Per Slice:	12.2

Sponge Cake

The fact that this cake worked as well as it does was bit of surprise, it will not rise to extreme heights, but does have a nice sponge texture. For those of you that don't like the taste of Splenda®, add the juice of a fresh lemon.

3/4 cup egg substitute eggs
1 cup Splenda®
4 tbsp. warm water
3/4 cup oat flour
1/4 cup gluten
2 tablespoon baking powder
1 teaspoon vanilla

Pre-heat your oven to 350 degrees. In a medium sized bowl, add egg substitute beat with hand mixer till it beings to thicken. Add Splenda and beat together 5 minutes more till the mixture begins to increase in volume. Add 4 tablespoons warm water and mix again 1 minute. Sift together oat flour, gluten and baking powder and stir lightly into wet ingredients, add the vanilla. Spread evenly in an 8 x 8 glass cake pan, sprayed lightly with cooking spray. Bake 20 minutes or until lightly brown, cut into 12 equal slices.

Calorie Count:	
Egg substitute –	90
Splenda® –	96
Oat Flour –	234
Gluten –	120
Baking Powder –	12
Vanilla –	12
Total	564
Per Slice:	47
Carbohydrates Count:	
Egg substitute –	6
Splenda® –	24
Oat Flour –	36
Gluten –	6
Baking Powder –	7.6
Vanilla –	0.5
Total	80.1
Per Slice:	6.7

Cherry Breakfast rolls

If you wish you can top these with about a half a teaspoon of frosting while they are still hot; it will add about 8 calories and 1.25 carbohydrates to each.

2 cups oat flour
3/4 cup gluten
1 cup Splenda®
2 tablespoons baking powder
1 teaspoons salt
1/4 cup egg substitute
1 cup water
1 can cherries packed in water chopped and well drained

Pre-heat the oven to 350 degrees. Combine the ingredients in the order listed and mix well. Spray two cookie sheets with cooking spray, spoon 1/3 cups of the mixture onto the cookie sheets and flatten into a circle about ½ inch high and 4 inches in rough diameter repeat till mixture is used up. Bake for 30 – 35 minutes, the recipe will make about 10 rolls

Calorie Count:	
Egg substitute –	30
Gluten –	360
Oat Flour –	624
Splenda® –	96
Cherry's	180
Baking Powder –	12
Total:	1302
Per Roll:	130.2
Carbohydrates Count:	
Egg substitute –	1
Gluten –	18
Oat Flour –	96
Splenda® –	24
Cherry's	42
Baking Powder –	7.6
Total:	188.6
Per Roll:	18.9

Cinnamon Orange Breakfast Sticks

The heat of the oven will cause the alcohol in the orange extract to evaporate, eliminating its calorie count.

1 3/8 cups water
1/4 cup egg substitute
1 teaspoon orange extract
1 teaspoon salt
1 tablespoon Spread
3/4 cup vital gluten
2 cups oat flour
1 tablespoon cinnamon
1/2 cup Splenda
2 tablespoons yeast

Pre-heat the oven to 350 degrees. Place into your bread machine in order listed and process in quick mode until kneading is complete. Remove the dough to a flat surface dusted with oat flour. Roll out into a rough square about 1/2 inches thick. With a very sharp knife cut i/2 inch strips about 8 inches long. Place on a cookie sheet cover and let rest for 10 minutes. Bake for about 25 minutes. This recipe will make 50 plus breakfast sticks.

Calorie Count:	
Egg substitute –	30
Gluten –	360
Oat Flour –	624
Splenda® –	48
Cinnamon –	34
Spread –	45
Total:	1141
Per Stick:	22.8
Carbohydrates Count:	
Egg substitute –	1
Gluten –	18
Oat Flour –	96
Splenda® –	12
Cinnamon –	11
Spread –	0
Total:	138
Per Stick:	2.8

Quick Breads

When I started these experiments one of the recipes that I wished to replicate was baking powder biscuits, my mother was an excellent biscuit maker, she began a lifelong love affair in me with these nuggets of goodness and I knew that I would continue to fail at any diet unless I had an acceptable substitute. It took nearly two years to get this particular recipe to point where I could consider it a substitute. Along the way I had to jettison some long held beliefs about what constituted a biscuit, for example that a biscuit had to be round. A very sharp knife will always beat biscuit cutter in creating good not crushed edges (crushed edges will deter the biscuit from rising), and, of course, there is far less waste cutting the biscuit this way, you don't have to reshape the left over dough into a new sheet to be re-cut, this always (in my experience) creates miss shaped and partly risen results.

A wheel of scones, waiting for a bit of Spread and a cup of coffee

Yogurt Biscuits

Very simple a case where a little goes a long way

2 cups oat flour
3/4 cup gluten
2 tablespoons baking powder
1 cup Yogurt

Pre-heat oven to 450 degrees, sift together the oat flour, gluten and baking powder. Add yogurt and mix till it just holds together. Sprinkle a bit of oat flout on a flat surface and dump the mixture onto it. Mead 10 or so times till combined and smooth. Pull together into a round shape about 1/2 inch thick cut (with biscuit cutter or knife) and place on a cookie sheet sprayed with a little cooking spray, reshape scraps and re-cut. Bake for about 20 minutes, makes about 9 biscuits.

Calorie Count:	
Baking powder –	12
Gluten –	360
Oat Flour –	624
Yogurt –	110
Total:	1106
Per biscuits:	122.9
Carbohydrates Count:	
Baking Powder –	7.6
Gluten –	18
Oat Flour –	96
Yogurt –	21
Total:	142.6
Per biscuits:	15.8

Pancakes

For a very interesting taste, add a little imitation maple flavor (such as Mapleine®) to the batter and put the syrup on the inside of the pancake.

¼ cup egg substitute
2 tablespoons Splenda®
2 cups water
½ cup vital wheat gluten
1 1/2 cups oat flour
2 tablespoon baking powder

In a large bowl beat egg substitute and Splenda® till they are very well mixed, add water and mix again, sift in the gluten, oat flour and mix until well incorporated. Bake on a hot griddle about 1/3 of a cup per pancake. This will make about 14 good size pancakes.

Calorie Count:	
Egg substitute –	30
Splenda® –	12
Gluten –	240
Oat Flour –	468
Baking powder –	12
Total:	762
Per pancake:	54.4
Carbohydrates Count:	
Egg substitute –	1
Splenda® –	3
Gluten –	12
Oat Flour –	72
Baking Powder –	7.6
Total:	95.6
Per pancake:	6.8

Waffles

Crispy on the outside yet soft on the inside almost the perfect waffle

3/4 cups oat flour
1/4 cup gluten
1 tablespoons baking powder
1 cup yogurt
1/2 cup egg substitute

Pre-heat your waffle iron; sift together the oat flour, gluten and baking powder. Add yogurt and egg substitute mix well (if too thick add a bit of water to thin). Bake a full 1/3 cup of the mixture in your waffle iron till steam stops coming out. Makes about 6 waffles

Calorie Count:	
Oat Flour –	234
Gluten –	120
Baking powder –	6
Yogurt –	110
Egg substitute –	60
Total:	530
Per Waffle:	88.3
Carbohydrates Count:	
Oat Flour –	36
Gluten –	6
Baking Powder –	3.8
Yogurt –	21
Egg substitute –	2
Total:	68.8
Per Waffle:	11.5

Basic Muffins

The American name for a type of bread baked in small portions, at least according to Wikipedia.

3/4 cups oat flour
1/4 cup gluten
½ cup Splenda®
2 tablespoons baking powder
1 cup yogurt
1/2 cup egg substitute

Pre-heat your oven to 350 degrees; sift together the oat flour, gluten and baking powder. Add yogurt, egg substitute and Splenda® mix well (if thick add a bit of water to thin), pour a full 1/3 cup of the mixture in muffin tins that have been sprayed with cooking spray and dusted with oat flour, or use paper muffin cups. Bake for about 30 minutes. Makes about 8 muffins

Calorie Count:	
Oat Flour –	234
Gluten –	120
Baking powder –	12
Yogurt –	110
Egg substitute –	60
Splenda® –	48
Total:	584
Per Muffin:	73.0
Carbohydrates Count:	
Oat Flour –	36
Gluten –	6
Baking Powder –	7.6
Yogurt –	21
Egg substitute –	2
Splenda® –	12
Total:	84.6
Per Muffin:	10.6

Scones

For an extra treat (that adds only a little extra calories and carbohydrates) sprinkle a package of raw sugar over the scones.

½ cup vital wheat gluten
1½ cups oat flour
2 tablespoon baking powder
2 tablespoons Splenda®
2 tablespoons Spread
¾ cup of water
¼ cup egg substitute

Pre-heat oven to 450 degrees, sift gluten oat flour baking powder and Splenda® in bowl mix very well. Add Spread and work it into the dry mixture until it has a crumbly look to it (I use a fork for this purpose). Add egg substitute and water. Mix until it comes away from the sides of the bowl (if to dry add just a bit of additional water). Place a little oat flour on a dry level surface dump the dough onto it, knead 12 times. Form into a ball and flatten to about ½ inch thick circle. With a sharp knife cut the dough in half then into quarters then eights, place on a cookie sheet that has been sprayed with cooking spray and bake for 12 minutes. Cool on a rack. This recipe will makes 8 Scones.

Calorie Count:	
Oat Flour –	468
Gluten –	240
Baking powder –	12
Splenda® –	12
Spread –	90
Egg substitute –	30
Total:	852
Per Scone:	106.5

Carbohydrates Count:	
Oat Flour –	72
Gluten –	12
Baking Powder –	7.6
Splenda® –	3
Spread –	0
Egg substitute –	1
Total:	95.6
Per Scone:	15.9

Basic Batter Bread

A whole new style of bread, well at least to me

1 ½ cups warm
1 tablespoon yeast
1 tablespoons Spread
1 tablespoon honey
1 teaspoon salt
2 cups oat flour
3/4 cup gluten

Pre-heat the oven to 350 degrees. Place all ingredients in a large bowl and mix with a hand mixture for 2 or 3 minutes it will become a thick batter. Spray a bread pan liberally with cooking spray and pour in the mixture, be sure to scrape as much of the material as possible from the bowl. Allow to rise for about an hour, or until double. Bake for 30 minutes turn out onto a cooling rack and allow to cool completely slice and serve make 18 ½ inch slices. As with all batter type breads, it is recommended that you use a non-stick bread pan.

Calorie Count:	
Spread –	45
Honey –	60
Gluten –	360
Oat Flour –	624
Total:	1089
Per Slice:	60.5
Carbohydrates Count:	
Spread –	0
Honey –	15
Gluten –	18
Oat Flour –	96
Total:	129
Per Slice:	7.2

Honey Cakes

Knife cut squares work well here as well, and feel a bit more traditional than those cut with a biscuit cutter.

1 cup egg substitute
2 tablespoons honey
2 cups oat flour
¾ cup vital gluten
¼ teaspoon salt
2 tablespoon Baking Powder
1 teaspoon allspice
Grated rind and juice of ½ lemon
1 tablespoon honey mixed with 1 tablespoon water

Pre-heat your oven to 350 degrees. Place the all material (except the honey water mixture) in your bread machine and set to quick mode (note- you may have to add a bit more oat flour to get the mixture to consolidate correctly, so check the progress of the kneading). Remove the dough after about 10 minutes of kneading. Dust a dry flat surface with oat flour and roll out a rectangle about ¼ inches in thickness and cut with a 2 1/2 inch biscuit cutter, re-roll and re-cut the scraps. Brush lightly with honey water mixture. Bake on a cookie sheet sprayed lightly with cooking spray, for 15 – 20 minutes or until lightly browned allow to cool completely on a cooling rack. This recipe will make 16 cakes.

Calorie Count:	
Egg substitute –	120
Honey –	120
Gluten –	360
Oat Flour –	624
Baking powder –	12
Allspice –	10
Honey –	60
Total:	1306
Per Cake:	81.6
Carbohydrates Count:	
Egg substitute –	4
Honey –	30
Gluten –	18
Oat Flour –	96
Baking Powder –	7.6
Allspice –	2
Honey –	15
Total:	172.6
Per Cake:	10.8

Banana Bread

Close your eyes and you can't tell the difference between this and the real thing. The banana extract is basically flavoring suspended in an alcohol base, the calories and carbohydrates are in the alcohol, which evaporates during baking

2 cups oat flour
3/4 cup gluten
1 1/2 cups warm water
1 tablespoons yeast
¼ cup Splenda Brown Sugar Blend®
1 tablespoon plus 1 teaspoon banana extract
1 tablespoon Spread
¼ cup egg substitute

Pre-heat the oven to 350 degrees. Place all materials in a large bowl and mix with a hand mixture for 2 or 3 minutes it will become a thick batter. Spray a bread pan with a good amount of cooking spray and pour in the mixture, be sure to scrape as much of the material as possible from the bowl. Allow to rise for about an hour, or until double. Bake for 30 minutes turn out onto a cooling rack and allow to cool completely, slice and serve this recipe makes 18 ½ inch slices. As with all batter type breads, it is recommended that you use a non-stick bread pan.

Calorie Count:	
Splenda Brown Sugar Blend® –	240
Gluten –	360
Oat Flour –	624
Banana extract –	4
Spread –	45
Egg substitute –	30
Total:	1303
Per slice:	72.4
Carbohydrates Count:	
Splenda Brown Sugar Blend® –	48
Gluten –	18
Oat Flour –	96
Banana extract –	0
Spread –	0
Egg substitute –	1
Total:	163
Per slice:	9.1

Baking Powder Biscuits

One of the last recipes I perfected also took the most time to adapt.

2 cups oat flour
3/4 cup vital gluten
2 tablespoons baking powder
1 teaspoon salt
4 tablespoons Spread
1 to 1 1/4 cups warm water

Pre-heat the oven to 400 degrees. Mix all of the dry ingredients add the Spread and cut it in with a fork until the material looks like corn meal i.e. grainy. Add the water and mix well, if needed adjust the dough with extra water or oat flour till you have soft sticky dough. Turn the dough out on a flat surface dusted well with oat flour and knead about 1 minute flatten into a rectangle about ½ inch thick and cut into squares about 2 inches square with a very sharp knife. Place on a cookie sheet that has been lightly sprayed with cooking spray and bake for 12 - 15 minutes. This recipe will produce about 20 biscuits.

Calorie Count:	
Gluten –	360
Oat Flour –	624
Baking Powder –	12
Spread –	180
Total:	1176
Per biscuit:	58.8
Carbohydrates Count:	
Gluten –	18
Oat Flour –	96
Baking Powder –	7.6
Spread –	0
Total:	121.6
Per biscuit:	6.1

Flat Bread

Prior to Egyptians (or whomever) discovering that yeast could make dough rise the world was eating bread as flat bread (what magic that must have been, a half inch high loaf becoming an inch high loaf). Even today there are many cultures that enjoy their bread as risen rounds rather than elongated loafs. I've always had an interest in this type of baking, in my wheat flour days I'd attempted making tortillas and pocket bread on a number of occasions so it was natural for me to bring these recipes along to this new media. The oat flour to gluten ratio was not a problem by the time I started on these recipes, but the amount of liquid was, the dough should be soft and a bit sticky, if too solid it will not rise properly and, for example, in the case of pocket bread will produce pizza shells not hollow loafs.

Pocket bread waiting of the fix'ens

Basic Flat Bread

Excellent bread for sandwiches split horizontally and stuff with your favorite sandwich fixing.

1 ½ cup of water
1 teaspoon salt
1 tablespoon Olive oil
1 tablespoon honey
1 tablespoon fat free dried milk
3/4 cup vital wheat gluten
2 cups oat flour
2 tablespoons yeast

Place the ingredients in your bread maker in the order stated in the recipe, run the machine through the knead cycle. Remove the dough and place on a surface that has been dusted with oat flour. Roll into a rope about 24 inches long and cut into 2 inch sections, the dough will be sticky. Roll out each section into a disk about 4 – 6 inches in diameter. Place on a surface well dusted with oat flour and allow to rise to double. Meanwhile pre-heat a griddle to high heat, when ready place on the heated griddle for about 8 minutes on a side. Don't overload your griddle with too many loafs, depending on its size 2 or 3 at a time is enough. Brush off the oat flour that clings to the loaf after they have cooled.

Calorie Count:	
Gluten –	360
Oat Flour –	624
Honey –	60
Olive Oil –	120
Dry Milk –	15
Total:	1179
Per loaf:	98.3
Carbohydrates Count:	
Gluten –	18
Oat Flour –	96
Honey –	15
Olive Oil –	15
Dry Milk –	2.25
Total:	146.25
Per loaf:	12.2

Tortillas

An oat flour variation of the Mexican staple

1 ¼ cups of water
1 teaspoon salt
1 tablespoons Spread
1/2 cup vital wheat gluten
2 cups oat flour

Add ingredients in order listed to bread machine, run machine in dough mode run it to mix and knead. When the machine switches to raise mode remove the dough. Lightly dust your working surface with oat flour. Roll the dough to a rope about 20 inches long and cut into 2 inch sections. Let rest while you heat your griddle (I use and electric griddle turned all the way up). Roll each section into a circle as thin as possible; you should be able to get them into a 6 inch or slightly larger circle. Place each tortilla on the griddle and cook each side till slightly brown the tortilla may puff slightly, this is expected. Remove to a dinner plate and cover with a kitchen towel. Repeat with remaining circles. This recipe will make about 10 Tortillas.

Calorie Count:	
Spread –	45
Gluten –	240
Oat Flour –	624
Total:	909
Per Tortilla:	90.9

Carbohydrates Count:	
Spread –	0
Gluten –	12
Oat Flour –	96
Total:	108
Per Tortilla:	10.8

Cinnamon cereal

The flattest of the flat breads, but oh so tasty

1 cup water
2 tablespoons Yogurt
1 teaspoon salt
½ cup Splenda®
½ cup vital wheat gluten
2 cups oat flour
1 heaping tablespoon of cinnamon

Pre-heat the oven to 375 degrees. Add ingredients in order listed to bread machine, run machine in dough mode run it to mix and knead. When the machine switches to raise mode remove the dough it should be very dense. Cut into 8 equal pieces. Roll out the sections as thin as possible (I use a pasta maker and roll it to the thinness possible thickness). Cut into 8 or so inch sections and place on a non-stick cookie sheet and bake in the middle of the oven for about 10 minutes. Remove from the oven and put on a rack to cool, repeat with the remainder of the dough. Once cooled break into serving size pieces, store in a sealed contain. This makes about 10 3/4 cup servings.

Calorie Count:	
Yogurt –	13.8
Splenda® –	48
Gluten –	240
Oat Flour –	624
Cinnamon –	17
Total:	942.8
Per Serving:	94.3

Carbohydrates Count:	
Yogurt –	2.6
Splenda® –	12
Gluten –	12
Oat Flour –	96
Cinnamon –	5.5
Total:	128.1
Per Serving:	12.8

Breakfast Flats

If you like, top with just a little frosting

1 ½ cups of water
1 teaspoon salt
¼ cup egg substitute
1 tablespoon Spread
1/4 cup Splenda brown sugar blend®
¼ cup
¾ cup vital gluten
2 cups oat flour
2 tablespoons cinnamon
2 tablespoon yeast

Place the ingredients into your bread machine in the order listed above, set your machine on quick bread setting and process. At the end of the cycle remove the dough and roll into a rectangle about 8 inches wide and 24 inches long, wet the top edge with a little water and roll up jelly roll fashion. Slice the dough into 1 inch sections, place on a surface dusted with oat four and allow to rise. Heat an electric griddle to low high (around 400 degrees), take each roll and flatten into a 4 or so inch circle with a rolling pin. Light spray the griddle with a non-stick cooking spray and quickly place the flattened rolls on the griddle, cook for about 8 minutes, flip, flatten and cook another 8 minutes, repeat with remaining rolls. Cool on a wire rack. This recipe will make about 24 rolls.

Calorie Count:	
Cinnamon –	34
Gluten –	360
Oat Flour –	624
Spread –	90
Splenda Brown Sugar Blend® –	240
Total:	1348
Per roll:	56.2
Carbohydrates Count:	
Cinnamon –	11
Gluten –	18
Oat Flour –	96
Spread –	0
Splenda Brown Sugar Blend® –	48
Total:	173
Per roll:	7.2

Focaccia

A 10 by 15 rectangle works excellent for this recipe as well, and will reduce both the calorie and carbohydrate counts pre slice.

1 ½ cups of water
1 teaspoon salt
1 tablespoon Spread
2 cups oat flour
3/4 cup gluten
1 tablespoon honey
1 teaspoon garlic powder
1 teaspoon dried oregano
1 teaspoon dried thyme
1/2 teaspoon dried basil
1 pinch ground black pepper
2 tablespoon yeast

Pre-heat your oven to 450 degrees. Place the ingredients into your bread machine in the order listed, set your machine on dough or quick bread setting and process until it goes into raise mode, remove the dough from the machine onto a counter space that has been dusted with a bit of oat flour, allow to rest for 5 minutes. Form into a round loaf about 12 inches in diameter and about ½ inch thick. Spray a baking sheet with a non-stick spray and place the loaf upon it. Spray the surface of the loaf lightly with non-stick cooking spray. Bake for about 15 – 20 minutes or until brown. Cut into 12 slices and serve warm.

Calorie Count:	
Spread –	45
Gluten –	360
Oat Flour –	624
Honey –	60
Spices –	18
Total:	1107
Per Slice:	92.3
Carbohydrates Count:	
Spread –	0
Gluten –	18
Oat Flour –	96
Honey –	15
Spices –	3.8
Total:	132.8
Per Slice:	11.1

Pocket Bread

One of my wife's favorite breads, she loves to stuff them with all sort of sandwich fixings.

1 ½ cups of water
1 tablespoon honey
2 tablespoons Spread
1 teaspoon salt
3/4 cup vital wheat gluten
2 cups oat flour
2 tablespoon yeast

Add ingredients in order listed to the bread machine run machine in dough mode and run it to mix and knead. When the machine switches to raise mode remove the dough to a flat clean surfaced dusted liberally with oat flour, the dough will be sticky. Roll into a rope about 26 inches long and cut into 2 inch slices. Roll each slice into a 6 inch circle.

Calorie Count:	
Gluten –	360
Oat Flour –	624
Honey –	60
Spread –	90
Total:	1134
Per loaf:	87.2
Carbohydrates Count:	
Gluten –	18
Oat Flour –	96
Honey –	15
Spread –	0
Total:	129
Per loaf:	9.9

Place on a surface dusted with oat flour, cover them with a light towel for about 1/2 hours (or until the loaves are puffy). Arrange your oven racks so that there is only one and it should be the bottom rack. Heat the oven to 500 degrees. When it reaches temperature place the loaves (one or two at a time) directly on the rack (a pizza stone works well too), bake for 3 - 4 minutes or until the tops are just brown and the loaf puffed remove to a rack and cover with a towel while they cool. Repeat with the remaining loaves. The recipe makes about 13 loafs. The ones that don't rise (which should be a rare occurrence) make great pizza shells.

Oat Flour Arepas

An Argentine staple made from oat flour instead of corn meal.

1 1/2 cup warm water
1 teaspoon olive oil
1 teaspoon salt
2 3/4 - 3 cups oat flour

Calorie Count:	
Oat Flour –	936
Olive Oil –	120
Total:	1056
Per loaf:	132.0
Carbohydrates Count:	
Oat Flour –	144
Olive Oil –	0
Total:	144
Per loaf:	18.0

Pre-heat your oven to 350 degrees, pre-heat your griddle to medium. Place water, salt and oil in a large bowl; add half the oat flour and mix. Add the remainder of the oat flour a bit at a time and knead in the bowl until you have a stiff slightly sticky dough. Cut the dough into 8 roughly equal pieces, roll each into a ball and flatten into a puck about an inch thick. Spray the griddle very lightly with cooking spray and place the loafs on the griddle and bake until the bottom is browned, about 10 minutes, flip and cook for a similar amount of time. Transfer to non-stick cookie sheet and place in the pre heated oven bake for 15 - 20 minutes.

White Salt Crackers

Warning!! These are addictive with or without a dip.

1 1/2 cups water
1/4 teaspoon salt
1 tablespoon fat fee dried milk
2 1/2 cups oat flour
1/2 cup vital gluten
Salt for the tops

Pre-heat the oven to 350 degrees put the ingredients into your bread machine in the order listed and process till the rise cycle starts. Remove the dough onto a surface well dusted with oat flour divide into quarters. Roll one of the quarters into a rectangle as thin as possible, sprinkle the surface with salt (the amount would be according to you own taste, I use a fair amount) and run your rolling pin over the surface of the dough to impress the salt into the dough. Cut into 2 inch strips and, using a fork, prick the surface of the dough well. Cut the strips into 2 inch squares. Place on a cookie sheet, bake for 9 minutes, remove and flip the crackers bake for another 9 minutes, be careful because they are so thin these can burn quickly. Move to a rack to cool, this recipe will make about 100 crackers.

Calorie Count:	
Gluten –	240
Oat Flour –	780
Dry Milk –	15
Total:	1035
Per Crackers:	10.4
Carbohydrates Count:	
Gluten –	12
Oat Flour –	120
Dry Milk –	2.25
Total:	134.25
Per Cracker:	1.3

Sourdough

Imagine my surprise, I was trying to make pancakes using the sponge method (a mixture of flour water and sugar left over night to ferment) when I review the results the next morning lo and behold I was looking at sourdough starter, I'd never even considered the possibility that some other material besides wheat could be used to create a starter (I've since learned about rye starters).
A few tips to keep your starter going:
Sourdough, if not supplemented with extra yeast, will rise far slower than most bread you are used to. Some of my recipes use sourdough as a flavoring agent, and this what you usually see in most recipes.
Feed each and every week or your starter can lose its potency. There are two basic ways to prepare you starter for use, the more traditional method would be to take the starter out of storage the morning before you plan to use it, allow its temperature to rise to room temperature. That evening replenish the starter as described in the starter recipe. This will give you the ultimate in sourdough flavor. However if what you are after is merely the ability to use the starter to rise bread, cakes etc. and do not mind a somewhat less sour taste, then follow this method. Remove the starter from storage; add equal amounts of oat flour and warm water and a teaspoon or so of honey. Allow to sit for 4 – 6 hours and use in your recipe. If you are not going to use your starter for a few weeks (heading for Maui for a two week vacation perhaps), freeze a couple of cups of starter, toss (or give away) the rest. Take this opportunity to clean your storage container. When you next wish to use the starter, remove it from the freezer and allow it to completely defrost. Place it in your jar and feed it using the traditional method discussed above.

Chive and Cracked Black Pepper Sourdough Batter Bread

Sourdough starter

This is the basic sourdough starter and is the center piece for the following recipes.

1 tablespoon of yeast
2 cup warm water
1 teaspoon salt
1 tablespoon honey
½ cup vital wheat gluten
1 1/2 cups oat flour

Mix yeast, water, salt and honey, sift in the gluten and oat flour and mix, and adjust with water till the mixture is slightly thick. Pour in a very clean large jar and cover with cheese cloth, allow to stand in a warm place for 2 or 3 days, after which it should be refrigerated, bring to room temperature to use. To replenish add equal amounts of oat flour and warm water with a teaspoon of honey, allow to set over night before storing it this recipe will provide 4 cups of sourdough for various recipes.

,

Calorie Count:	
Honey –	60
Gluten –	240
Oat Flour –	468
Total:	768
Per cup:	192.0
Carbohydrates Count:	
Honey –	15
Gluten –	12
Oat Flour –	72
Total:	99
Per cup:	24.8

Sourdough Bread

This is excellent tasting sourdough bread that uses the sourdough as a flavoring agent.

1 cup sourdough starter
1/2 cup lukewarm water
1 tablespoon Honey
1 tablespoon Spread
1/2 teaspoon salt
2 cups oat flour
3/4 cup vital wheat gluten
1/8 teaspoon baking soda
2 tablespoon yeast

Prepare your starter in one of the two methods described elsewhere. Pre-heat oven to 350 degrees, add ingredients in order to bread machine set to quick dough mode and run it to mix and knead. Remove the dough from the machine and place on a flat surface that has been dusted with a bit of oat flour and roll it up tightly, place in a bread pan sprayed with a bit of cooking spray. Cover and allow to rise in a warm place until doubled, bake for 25 - 30 minutes. Remove from the oven and place on cooling rack. Makes 18 ½ inch slices

Calorie Count:	
Starter –	192
Gluten –	360
Oat Flour –	624
Honey –	60
Spread –	45
Total:	1281
Per slice:	71.2
Carbohydrates Count:	
Starter –	24.8
Gluten –	18
Oat Flour –	96
Honey –	15
Spread –	0
Total:	153.8
Per slice:	8.5

Sourdough Pancakes

This makes an outstanding pancake thin, light and with a great sourdough taste.

1 cup sourdough starter
3/4 cup oat flour
¼ cup vital gluten
1 cup warm water
¼ cup egg substitute
1 tablespoon Spread
1 tablespoon Honey
1/2 teaspoon salt
1/2 teaspoon baking soda

The evening before place the starter, oat flour, gluten and water in a large glass or ceramic bowl mix well and cover loosely. In the morning add the rest of the ingredients and mix adjust the mixture with oat flour or water to make a slightly thick batter. On a very hot griddle pour ¼ cup of the mixture for each pancake. This recipe will make about 18 pancakes.

Calorie Count:	
Starter –	192.0
Egg substitute –	30
Gluten –	120
Oat Flour –	234
Honey –	60
Spread –	45
Soda –	0
Total:	681
Per pancake:	37.8
Carbohydrates Count:	
Starter –	24.8
Egg substitute –	1
Gluten –	6
Oat Flour –	36
Honey –	15
Spread –	0
Soda –	0
Total:	82.75
Per pancake:	4.6

Sourdough Biscuits

There is no law that says that a biscuit has to be round; I often use this technique rather than using a biscuit cutter just be sure you use a very sharp knife.

2 cups sourdough starter
2 tablespoons Spread
1 ½ cups of oat flour
½ cup gluten
1 teaspoon salt
1/8 teaspoon baking soda
1 tablespoon Honey

Prepare your starter in one of the two methods described elsewhere. The next morning pre-heat your oven to 425 degrees. Mix all of the ingredients in a large bowl until you have medium soft dough, dust the working surface with a bit of oat flour roll out the mixture and knead 10 to 12 times. Roll or pat the dough into a square about ½ inches thick. Cut into 2 inch squares and place on a cookie sheet sprayed lightly with cooking spray. Set in a warm place and let rise for an hour or until very light. Bake for 15 – 20 minutes, with careful slicing you should get 20 biscuits from this recipe.

Calorie Count:	
Starter –	384
Gluten –	240
Oat Flour –	468
Honey –	60
Spread –	90
Soda –	0
Total:	1242
Per biscuit:	62.1
Carbohydrates Count:	
Starter –	49.5
Gluten –	12
Oat Flour –	72
Honey –	15
Spread –	0
Soda –	0
Total:	148.5
Per biscuit:	7.4

Sourdough French bread

In this recipe the sourdough is not used as a flavoring agent, here it is front and center as the means of leavening, be patient, sourdough works at its own pace.

1 cup sourdough starter
3/4 cup warm water
1 tablespoon honey
1 teaspoons salt
1/2 teaspoon baking soda
2 cups oat flour
3/4 cup vital gluten

Prepare your starter in one of the two methods described elsewhere. Pre-heat the oven to 375 degrees. Put the ingredients in your bread machine in the order listed and run the machine in quick mode, to mix and knead. Spray the cookie sheet very lightly with cooking spray. Dust your work surface with a bit of oat flour and pour out the dough, knead and shape into a French bread shape about 14 inches long. Slice diagonally with a very sharp knife, do not slice deeply. Allow the rise till double in volume (this could take several hours depending on the strength of you starter) sprinkle the top with water. Boil 1 cup of water (microwave is fine), place in a pan in the pre-heated oven, add the dough and bake for about 25 minutes. This recipe will make 28 ½ inch thick slices.

Calorie Count:	
Starter –	192.0
Gluten –	360
Oat Flour –	624
Honey –	60
Soda –	0
Total:	1236
Per slice:	44.1
Carbohydrates Count:	
Starter –	24.8
Gluten –	18
Oat Flour –	96
Honey –	15
Soda –	0
Total:	153.75
Per Slice:	5.5

Sourdough Hot Dog Buns

Great for hot dogs, but big enough to be used as a hoagie roll as well

1 cup sourdough starter
3/4 cup warm water
1 tablespoon honey
1 teaspoons salt
1/2 teaspoon baking soda
2 cups oat flour
3/4 cup vital gluten
1 tablespoon yeast

Prepare your starter in one of the two methods described elsewhere. Pre-heat the oven to 350 degrees. Put the ingredients in your bread machine in the order listed and run the machine in quick mode, to mix and knead. Spray the cookie sheet very lightly with cooking spray. Dust your work surface with a bit of oat flour and pour out the dough. Cut the dough in half and then each half in half continue until you have 8 roughly equal pieces. Roll each piece into a tube about 6 inches in length. Place the tubes on a cookie sheet sprayed with a bit of cooking spray and allow too rise until double in bulk. Bake for about 30 minutes. Move to a cool rack and allow cooling completely, split each bun about ¾ the way through. Note- for a more normal size bun cut the dough into 12 equal pieces, this will also bring the calorie and carbohydrate count down.

Calorie Count:	
Starter –	192.0
Gluten –	360
Oat Flour –	624
Honey –	60
Soda –	0
Total:	1236
Per Bun:	154.5
Carbohydrates Count:	
Starter –	24.8
Gluten –	18
Oat Flour –	96
Honey –	15
Soda –	0
Total:	153.75
Per Bun:	19.2

Sourdough Muffins

Muffins with the slight tang of sourdough are interesting enough to not need frosting.

1/2 cup egg substitute
2 teaspoon vanilla
1/2 teaspoon salt
1/2 cup yogurt
2 ¼ cups sourdough starter
1 1/2 cup oat flour
1/2 cup vital wheat gluten
2 tablespoons cinnamon
1 teaspoon baking soda
1/2 cup Splenda®

Prepare your starter in one of the two methods described elsewhere. Pre-heat oven to 425 degrees, sift together the dry ingredients in medium bowl. Wisk together the wet ingredients in a separate large bow, allow this mixture to sit for ½ hours. Add dry ingredients to wet ones. Spray your non-stick muffin tins with a bit of cooking spray and fill to about 2/3 full with the mixture. Bake about 20 minutes, makes about 18 muffins.

Calorie Count:	
Egg substitute –	60
Starter –	432
Gluten –	240
Oat Flour –	468
Splenda® –	48
Yogurt –	55
Soda –	0
Cinnamon –	34
Vanilla –	24
Total:	1337
Per Muffin:	74.3
Carbohydrates Count:	
Egg substitute –	2
Starter –	55.69
Gluten –	12
Oat Flour –	72
Splenda® –	12
Yogurt –	10.5
Soda –	0
Cinnamon –	11
Vanilla –	1
Total:	175.19
Per Muffin:	9.7

Sourdough Vanilla Cake

The scraping of the inside of the vanilla bean adds no actual calories or carbohydrates to this cake.

1/2 cup egg substitute
2 teaspoon vanilla
1/2 teaspoon salt
1/2 cup yogurt
2 1/4 cups sourdough starter
1 vanilla bean, scraped
1 1/2 cup oat flour
1/2 cup vital wheat gluten
1 teaspoon baking soda
1/2 cup Splenda®

Prepare your starter in one of the two methods described elsewhere. Pre-heat oven to 400 degrees, sift together the dry ingredients in medium bowl. Wisk together the wet ingredients (along with the vanilla bean scrapings) in a separate large bow, allow this mixture to sit for ½ hours. Add dry ingredients to wet ones and mix. Spray a 9 by 13 inch cake pan with a bit of cooking spray and evenly add the mixture. Bake about 30 minutes; makes about 24, 2 inch square slices. The cake may be frosted with one of the frosting recipe found elsewhere in the book, factor in the calories and carbohydrates.

Calorie Count:	
Egg substitute –	60
Starter –	432
Gluten –	240
Oat Flour –	468
Splenda® –	48
Yogurt –	55
Soda –	0
Vanilla –	24
Total:	1327
Per Slice:	55.3
Carbohydrates Count:	
Egg substitute –	2
Starter –	33.75
Gluten –	12
Oat Flour –	72
Splenda® –	12
Yogurt –	10.5
Soda –	0
Vanilla –	1
Total:	143.25
Per Slice:	6.0

Sourdough Chocolate Cake

This is an amazing cake, server it to someone who doesn't know its limited in calories and carbohydrates and they would not know the difference.

1/2 cup egg substitute
2 teaspoons vanilla
1/2 teaspoon salt
1/2 cup yogurt
2 1/2 cups sourdough starter
¼ cup Cocoa powder
1 1/2 cup oat flour
1/2 cup vital wheat gluten
1 teaspoon baking soda
1/2 cup Splenda®

Prepare your starter in one of the two methods described elsewhere. Pre-heat oven to 400 degrees, sift together the dry ingredients in medium bowl. Wisk together the wet ingredients in a separate large bow, allow this mixture to sit for ½ hours. Add dry ingredients to wet ones and mix well. Spray a 9 by 13 inch cake pan with a bit of cooking spray and evenly add the mixture. Bake about 30 minutes; makes about 24, 2 inch square slices. The cake may be frosted with one of the frosting recipe found elsewhere in the book, factor in the calories and carbohydrates.

Calorie Count:	
Starter –	480
Gluten –	240
Oat Flour –	468
Splenda® –	48
Yogurt –	55
Soda –	0
Cocoa powder–	80
Egg substitute –	60
Vanilla –	24
Total:	1371
Per slice:	57.1
Carbohydrates Count:	
Starter –	61.88
Gluten –	12
Oat Flour –	72
Splenda® –	12
Yogurt –	10.5
Soda –	0
Cocoa powder–	8
Egg substitute –	2
Vanilla –	1
Total:	176.38
Per Slice:	7.3

Sourdough Deep fry batter

This is excellent in the preparation of onion rings.

1 cup sourdough starter
¼ cup egg substitute
1 tablespoon olive oil
Pinch of salt
Pinch of pepper
About ¼ cup Oat flour

Prepare your starter in one of the two methods described elsewhere. Combine first 5 ingredients add oat flour to make a thick batter of too thick add just a bit of water, beat for 1 or 2 minutes, let sit for 1 hour. Use to coat veggies for deep frying.

Calorie Count:	
Starter –	192.0
egg substitute –	30
Oat Flour –	78
Olive Oil –	120
Total:	420
Carbohydrates Count:	
Starter –	24.8
egg substitute –	1
Oat Flour –	12
Olive Oil –	0
Total:	37.8

Sourdough Pizza Crust

Pizza does not have to be round to be pizza, try making it into a rectangle on a cookie sheet.

1 1/2 cups sourdough starter
1 Tablespoon olive oil
1 teaspoon Salt
1 cup oat flour
½ cup vital gluten

Prepare your starter in one of the two methods described elsewhere. Pre-heat oven to 450 degrees; add ingredients to your bread machine in the order listed. Run the machine for about 8 minutes. Remove from the machine to a clean dry surface dusted with oat flour and roll into a circle as thin as you like. Add your favorite toppings and bake for about 18 minutes. This recipe will make about 24 slices of pizza, 2 inch square. Note the calorie and carbohydrate calculations are for the crust only.

Calorie Count:	
Starter –	288
Gluten –	240
Oat Flour –	312
Olive Oil –	120
Total:	960
Per Slice:	40.0
Carbohydrates Count:	
Starter –	37.13
Gluten –	12
Oat Flour –	48
Olive Oil –	0
Total:	97.13
Per Slice:	4.0

Sourdough Doughnuts

Some may think that sourdough doughnut might be an acquired taste, let me assure you that you will acquire a taste for these gems fairly quickly.

1 cup sourdough starter
1/2 cup Splenda
1/4 teaspoon Soda
¼ cup egg substitute
1/4 cup yogurt
1 1/2 cups oat flour
½ cup vital gluten
1/2 teaspoon Baking powder
1/2 teaspoon Cinnamon

Prepare your starter in one of the two methods described elsewhere. Place in order into you bread machine, place in quick mode for about 10 minutes, or until lightly kneaded. Dust your work surface with oat flour, remove the dough to this surface and roll to about 3/8 of an inch thick. Use a 2 ½ inch doughnut cutter, cut, re-roll the holes and leftovers (unless of course you like the holes) and continue cutting. Leave the doughnuts on the work surface lightly covered and allow to rise for at least an hour (two or more might be required). Heat your oil to 370 degrees and fry till brown on both sides, about 2 ½ minutes per side, place on paper towels to absorber any excess oil. These are great with a tablespoon or so of peanut honey frosting drizzled over the top. This recipe will make about 12 doughnuts.

Calorie Count:	
Starter –	192.0
egg substitute –	30
Oat Flour –	468
Gluten –	240
Splenda® –	48
Yogurt –	27.5
Soda –	0
Cinnamon –	2.83
Baking Powder –	1.0
Total:	1009.3
Per Doughnut:	84.11
Carbohydrates Count:	
Starter –	24.8
egg substitute –	1
Oat Flour –	72
Gluten –	12
Splenda® –	12
Yogurt –	5.25
Soda –	0
Cinnamon –	0.92
Baking Powder –	0.6
Total:	128.55
Per Doughnut:	10.7

Chive and Cracked Black Pepper Sourdough Batter Bread

One teaspoon of cracked black pepper will give a light peppery taste; a tablespoon will is somewhat over powering.

2 cups sourdough starter
1 cup warm water
1 tablespoon Honey
1 tablespoon Spread
1 teaspoon salt
2 cups oat flour
¾ cup vital gluten
1 teaspoon baking soda
1 tablespoon yeast
1 teaspoon cracked black pepper
¼ cup finely chopped fresh chives

Prepare your starter in one of the two methods described elsewhere. Pre-heat the oven to 375 degrees. In a large bowl shift in the oat flour and gluten, add the salt, honey, Spread, warm water, yeast and soda beat with a hand mixer for about 2 minutes. Add the black pepper, hand mix this till incorporated, adjust with warm water if necessary to achieve the thick batter. Spray a bread pan with cooking spray and add the batter, place in a warm place and allow to rise till it is just over the lip of the baking pan (this could take some time, do be patient, the dough will rise some while in bakes). Bake for 45 to 50 minutes, make 18 ½ in slices. As with all batter type breads, it is recommended that you use a non-stick bread pan.

Calorie Count:	
Starter –	384
Honey –	60
Spread –	45
Oat Flour –	624
Gluten –	360
Black Pepper –	16
Chives –	4
Soda –	0
Total:	1493
Per Slice:	82.9
Carbohydrates Count:	
Starter –	49.5
Honey –	15
Spread –	0
Oat Flour –	96
Gluten –	18
Black Pepper –	4.1
Chives –	0.4
Soda –	0
Total:	183
Per Slice:	10.2

Sourdough Crumpets

Unlike pancakes these are thick and cooked slowly, so watch the temperature of your griddle.

1 cups sourdough starter
1 1/2 cup warm water
1 tablespoon honey
1 tablespoon Spread
1/2 teaspoon salt
1 cups oat flour
1/2 cup vital gluten
1/2 teaspoon baking soda
1 tablespoon yeast

Prepare your starter in one of the two methods described elsewhere. Pre-heat a griddle place all of the ingredients into a large bowl and mix with a hand mixer for 2 or 3 minutes (this will condition the gluten properly) adjust with water or oat flour to achieve a thick batter. Prepare your muffin ring by greasing the sides with a small amount of Spread. Place on the griddle and allow to heat. Pour 1/3 of a cup of the mixture into each ring and allow to cook for about 5 or 6 minutes. Carefully, using a pair of tongs remove the rings and flip the crumpets, cook for another 5 or 6 minutes and then move to a cooling rack and let cool completely. After the rings have cooled, apply more Spread and repeat the cooking process. This recipe will produce about 8 crumpets.

Calorie Count:	
Starter –	192
Gluten –	240
Oat Flour –	312
Honey –	60
Soda –	0
Spread –	45
Total:	849
Per Crumpet:	106.1
Carbohydrates Count:	
Starter –	24.8
Gluten –	12
Oat Flour –	48
Honey –	15
Soda –	0
Spread –	0
Total:	99.8
Per Crumpet:	12.5

Extra

This chapter contains a number of recipes that don't fit well in any of the other categories in this book, as a matter of fact I consider for some time if I should include them at all. In the end I couldn't resist the temptation to include them, they are just too darn good to ignore, especially the pudding recipes. When I figured out how to make oat milk (and by the way this oat milk tends not to separate like some other I've tried) I almost immediately thought of trying to make a pudding, but figured that it wouldn't work, but one evening while suffering a major sugar attack I decided to give it a try. I knew that the oat milk was already fairly thick (I have a different recipe I us for drinking) and that the addition of just a bit more oat flour and the inclusion of some egg substitute (egg being a major thickening agent), should give me what I wanted. Low and behold it work, and on the very first try, one of the very few recipes here within to which that statement can be said. All of the oat milk recipes use the cooking variation not the drinking one.

Noodles drying on my homemade drying rack

Vanilla Frosting

1 8 oz. container of fat free Cream Cheese
4 tablespoon of Spread
1 tablespoon vanilla
2 tablespoons Splenda Brown Sugar Blend®

Bring the cream cheese and Spread to room temperature. Place all ingredients in a small bowl and mix with a hand mixer for 3 minutes. Store in your refrigerator, anything you use this mixture should also be refrigerated and covered.

Calorie Count:	
Fat Free Cream Cheese –	240
Spread –	180
Splenda Brown Sugar Blend® –	120
Vanilla –	12
Total:	552

Carbohydrates Count:	
Fat Free Cream Cheese –	16
Spread –	0
Splenda Brown Sugar Blend® –	24
Vanilla –	0.5
Total:	40.5

Peanut butter Honey Frosting

The top calorie and carbohydrate is for peanut butter, the bottom is for almond butter.

¼ cup honey
4 tablespoons Spread
½ cup reduced sugar peanut butter

Heat honey and Spread in a small sauce pan till it just starts to boil. Remove from the heat and add the peanut butter mix until very smooth, pour over the still warm cake. As an option that will reduce the calories and give an interesting taste, replace the peanut butter with almond butter.

Calorie Count:	
Spread –	180
Honey –	240
Peanut butter –	800
Total:	1220
Per slice:	50.8
Carbohydrates Count:	
Spread –	0
Honey –	60
Peanut butter –	20
Total:	80
Per Slice:	3.3

Calorie Count:	
Spread –	180
Honey –	240
Almond butter –	520
Total:	940
Per slice:	39.2
Carbohydrates Count:	
Spread –	0
Honey –	60
Almond butter –	20
Total:	80
Per Slice:	3.3

Egg noodles

This recipe reminds me of buckwheat noodles.

1 cup eggs substitute
1 teaspoon salt
1/2 cup vital gluten
1 1/2 cups oat flour

Sift together the salt, gluten and oat flour; add the egg substitute. Turn out onto a flat surface dusted with oat flour; knead until soft and not sticky. Rap and place in the refrigerator for at least 3 hours. Cut into 8 pieces. Using a pasta maker roll each piece as thin as possible finally cut (with the pasta machine) into the desired shape (spaghetti, noodles etc.). If you do not have a pasta maker roll your dough out into a rectangle as thin as you can, and cut into the shape you desire with a very sharp knife. This recipe will make 8 servings. Cook these by boiling in salted water until tender; they may be dried for later usage.

Calorie Count:	
Egg substitute –	120
Gluten –	240
Oat Flour –	468
Total:	828
Per Serving:	103.5
Carbohydrates Count:	
Egg substitute –	4
Gluten –	12
Oat Flour –	72
Total:	88
Per Serving:	11.0

Chili Gravy

This is great served over baking powder biscuits, or even just bread.

2 cups of water
1 tablespoon of Chili base
¼ cup of oat flour

Place the water into a medium size pan and add the oat flour, mix with a hand mixer till very smooth, add the chili base and whisk to mix. Put over high heat and bring to a boil, keep whisking to prevent it burning. You may have to lift the pot off the heat to prevent it from boiling over; when thick it is ready to serve. This recipe will make about 9 ¼ cup servings. Chicken, turkey or beef base may be used as well, check the calorie and carbohydrate counts and adjust (my chili base has 35 calorie and 2 carbohydrates per teaspoon).

Calorie Count:	
Chili base –	220
Oat Flour –	78
Total:	259
Per serving:	28.78

Carbohydrates Count:	
Chili base –	6
Oat Flour –	12
Total:	12
Per serving:	1.33

Oat Milk Drinking

A favorite of the folk in Sweden

4 cups of water
3 tablespoons of oat flour

Place the water and oat flour in a 2 quart or larger pot, whisk the mixture well (or mix with a electric hand mixer). Turn on the heat and bring to a boil whisking all the time. Boil for about 30 seconds, you will need to continue whisking and as it boils up pick the pot off the heat, else it will boil over and create a mess. Pour into a clean quart jar and allow to cool, any globs of oat flour that float to the surface, remove them with a spoon. Once cooled refrigerate, this recipe will make 4 1 cup servings.

Calorie Count:	
Oat Flour –	58.5
Total:	58.5
Per serving:	14.63
Carbohydrates Count:	
Oat Flour –	9
Total:	9
Per serving:	2.25

Oat Milk Cooking

A thicker version of oat milk ideal for cooking

5 cups of water
1/3 cup of oat flour

Place the water and oat flour in a 2 quart or larger pot, whisk the mixture well. Turn on the heat and bring to a boil whisking all the time. Boil for about 30 seconds, you will need to continue whisking and as it boils up pick the pot off the heat, it will boil over and create a mess. Allow to cool and refrigerate. This will produce fairly thick milk, nearly cream like. This recipe will make 5 1 cup servings.

Calorie Count:	
Oat Flour –	102.96
Total:	102.96
Per serving:	20.59
Carbohydrates Count:	
Oat Flour –	15.84
Total:	15.84
Per serving:	3.17

Oat Milk Whipped Cream

I find the amount of Splenda® just right in this recipe; you may find it a bit sweet.

2 cups oat milk cooking
1/3 cup no fat dried milk (for flavor)
1 cup cold water
3 packets of unflavored gelatin
1 teaspoon vanilla
½ cup Splenda®

Combine the cold water gelatin and vanilla, place in the microwave (or heat slowly over a low flame) till boiling remove and allow starting to cool. Place the oat milk and dried milk in a large bowl add the Splenda® begin to beat. Slowly add the water gelatin mixture and beat for 10 minutes (or until it has cooled and started to thicken and foam is starting to pile up). Pour into a bowl, cover and place into the refrigerator. Every 10 minutes or so, using a spoon, remix the foam back into the mixture. This recipe will make about 12 quarter cup severing.

Calorie Count:	
Oat Milk –	41.18
Dried Milk –	79.95
Splenda® –	48
Vanilla –	12
Gelatin –	60
Total:	241.13
Per serving:	20.09
Carbohydrates Count:	
Oat Milk –	6.34
Dried Milk –	11.99
Splenda® –	12
Vanilla –	0.5
Gelatin –	0
Total:	30.83
Per serving:	2.57

Quick Oat Milk Pudding

Use your favorite pudding mix, adjust the calorie and carbohydrate counts accordingly, you cannot tell the difference between this and one made from regular milk.

2 cups oat milk cooking
1 box instant pudding mix

Prepare as directed on the box, using oat milk instead of cows' milk. Make 4 ½ cup servings.

Calorie Count:	
Oat Milk –	41.18
pudding Mix –	100
Total:	141.18
Per serving:	35.30
Carbohydrates Count:	
Oat Milk –	6.34
pudding Mix –	24
Total:	30.34
Per serving:	7.58

Oat Milk Ice Cream

A bit more like a sorbet and ice cream cross, but a better choice over the real thing.

2 cups oat milk cooking
½ cup egg substitute
½ cup Splenda®
1 tablespoon vanilla

Mix together all ingredients in a 4 cup measuring cup (makes it easier to pour), pour into your ice cream machine process the mixture until very thick. Place into a freezer proof container and pop into the freezer. When serving, remove to the refrigerator for 15 minutes or so to soften. The recipe will make about 4 ½ cup servings.

Calorie Count:	
Oat Milk –	41.18
Splenda® –	48
Vanilla –	12
Egg substitute –	60
Total:	161.18
Per serving:	40.30
Carbohydrates Count:	
Oat Milk –	6.34
Splenda® –	12
Vanilla –	0.5
Egg substitute –	2
Total:	20.84
Per serving:	5.21

Stove Top Oat Milk Vanilla Custard

2 cups oat milk cooking
¾ cup egg substitute
½ cup Splenda®
1 tablespoon vanilla
¼ cup oat flour

Whisk together well all ingredients in a.2 quart pan if lumps remain use an electric mixer to achieve a smooth mixture, place over heat and continue to whisk while the mixture comes to a boil. Reduce the heat and cook for 2 minutes keep whisking while the mixture cooks. Move to bowl and allow to cool, cover and move to the refrigerator for at least 2 hours. The recipe will make about 6 ½ cup servings.

Calorie Count:	
Oat Milk –	41.18
Splenda® –	48
Vanilla –	36
Egg substitute –	90
Oat Flour –	78
Total:	293.18
Per serving:	48.86
Carbohydrates Count:	
Oat Milk –	6.34
Splenda® –	12
Vanilla –	1.5
Egg substitute –	3
Oat Flour –	12
Total:	34.84
Per serving:	5.81

Oat Milk Butterscotch Pudding

My favorite flavor of pudding, but prepared only as a treat because of the higher calorie and carbohydrate count.

2 cups oat milk cooking
½ cup egg substitute
¼ cup Splenda Brown Sugar Blend®
1 tablespoon Spread
¼ cup oat flour
¼ cup Splenda Brown Sugar Blend®

Whisk together well all ingredients (except Spread) in 2 quart pan, use an electric hand mixer if there are lumps remaining place over heat and continue to whisk while the mixture comes to a boil, reduce the heat and cook for 2 minutes, keep whisking. Remove the pan from the heat and add the Spread, keep whisking until the Spread is melted and completely incorporated. Move to bowl and allow to cool, cover and move to the refrigerator for at least 2 hours. When cool add the second ¼ cup of Splenda® and mix well. The recipe will make about 6 ½ cup servings

Calorie Count:	
Oat Milk –	41.18
Splenda Brown sugar Blend® –	240
Spread –	30
Egg substitute –	60
Oat Flour –	78
Splenda Brown sugar Blend® –	240
Total:	689.18
Per serving:	114.86
Carbohydrates Count:	
Oat Milk –	6.34
Splenda Brown sugar Blend® –	48
Spread –	1
Egg substitute –	2
Oat Flour –	12
Splenda Brown sugar Blend® –	48
Total:	117.34
Per serving:	19.56

Oat Milk Chocolate Pudding

Serve with a dollop of oat flour whipped cream on top.

2 cups oat milk cooking
½ cup egg substitute
½ cup Splenda®
¼ cup Cocoa powder
¼ cup oat flour

Whisk together well all ingredients in a.2 quart pan, be sure all lumps have been whisked out or use an electric hand mixer to achieve a smooth mixture, place over heat and continue to whisk while the mixture comes to a boil. Reduce the heat and cook for 2 minutes keep whisking while cooking. Move to bowl and allow to cool, cover and move to the refrigerator for at least 2 hours. The recipe will make about 6 ½ cup servings.

Calorie Count:	
Oat Milk –	41.18
Splenda® –	48
Cocoa powder –	80
Egg substitute –	60
Oat Flour –	78
Total:	307.18
Per serving:	51.20
Carbohydrates Count:	
Oat Milk –	6.34
Splenda® –	12
Cocoa powder –	8
Egg substitute –	2
Oat Flour –	12
Total:	40.34
Per serving:	6.72

Oat Milk Banana Pudding

Add a drop or 2 of yellow food coloring, it enhances the banana experience. Cooking evaporates the alcohol in the banana extract.

2 cups oat milk cooking
½ cup egg substitute
½ cup Splenda®
1 tablespoon Banana extract
¼ cup oat flour

Pour the oat milk into a 2 quart pan and add the other ingredients, whisk until there are no lumps (or use a hand mixer) turn the heat on high and heat to a boil and cook for 1 or 2 minutes whisk continuously while cooking, pour into a bowl and allow to cool, refrigerate until cold (at least an hour) and serve. This recipe will make about 5, ½ cup servings.

Calorie Count:	
Oat Milk –	41.18
Splenda® –	48
Egg substitute –	60
Oat Flour –	78
Total:	227.18
Per serving:	45.44
Carbohydrates Count:	
Oat Milk –	6.34
Splenda® –	12
Egg substitute –	2
Oat Flour –	12
Total:	32.34
Per serving:	6.47

Made in United States
Troutdale, OR
11/11/2024

24657189R00060